AGING WITH DIGNITY

LIVING WITH GRACE

8 STEPS TO HELP YOU OVERCOME ADVERSITY, FIND PEACE OF MIND AND PROSPERITY IN THE SECOND HALF OF LIFE

BY DAVID H. BRADY

"Aging with Dignity, Living with Grace," by David H. Brady. ISBN 978-1-62137-474-9 (softcover).

Library of Congress Number: 2014904681

Published 2014 by Virtualbookworm.com Publishing Inc., P.O. Box 9949, College Station, TX 77842, US. ©2014, David H. Brady. All rights reserved. No part of this publication may be reproduced, stored in a retrieval system, or transmitted in any form or by any means, electronic, mechanical, recording or otherwise, without the prior written permission of David H. Brady.

Manufactured in the United States of America.

Cover photo by David Kastner.

David H. Brady, MFA
505-1550 Duchess Avenue
West Vancouver, BC
(613) 484 9675

Email: david@davidbradyproductions.com

In loving memory of my Mother.

-ACKNOWLEDGMENTS-

I would like to thank my long-suffering family and friends who've all pitched in to help me, thanks Bev.

A special thanks to Tierney Ness and her good friend and trusty sailing partner Barry Devonald, and without whose help and guidance this book would be a dog's breakfast, thank you. They really forced me to grow as both a writer and a human being. Thank you both.

I want to thank my oldest friends in the world, Mike O'Shea and Brian Rogers for their undying support and kindness.

Thanks to my new pals Kumar, Bert, Peter and Tom and Dr. Mike for being willing to give me honest feedback.

Thanks to my new Master Mind partners, Mike, Barb, and Jey and Tierney.

A very special thanks to my old friends Alan Vogeler, George Flak and Richard Landry.

A very special thanks to my business associate Sonny Goldstein and the incredible help he's been.

Last but not least thanks to the folks at Virtualbookworm for their support.

-FOREWORD-

In the late spring of 2013, I was faced with one of the most difficult situations of my adult life. It appeared that in the first week of July, I might lose everything I'd worked so hard to build up in the previous thirty years.

On January 4th, 2010 I had stopped by a woman's home to speak to her son at her request. It turns out that the young man was suffering from severe mental illness. Without warning, while I was sitting in a chair, he punched me so hard I flew through the air, landed on my back and then found him on top of me with my arms pinned under his legs while he drove about six or seven rage filled punches into my head sending my skull smashing into the solid hardwood kitchen floor. It was surreal as his face, and every punch came into focus in slow motion. Just before I went unconscious I said, "What are you doing?" At that moment, I could see in his eyes, there was no one home. He was completely psychotic.

He was 22 yeas old, over six feet tall and by his own admission in a letter to me, worked out two to three hours a day trying to control the voices in his head.

When I got free I ran out of the house and in a state of shock, my hands shaking uncontrollably, my mind racing, I jumped in the car I'd had just driven non stop from Florida to Toronto over 30 hours and ended up driving for another two hours to try and get to my house in Eastern Ontario, where I felt I would be safe, only to end up in a hospital, where they diagnosed me with a concussion.

My face, head and skull showed significant trauma. The result of that incident: I have brain damage that has dramatically impacted every aspect of my life; impaired my ability to do the work I've done all of my career and left me wondering, how do I overcome these challenges? The bottom line – this assault has altered the direction of my life permanently.

I'm grateful to say that as a result of meeting a wonderful physician, Dr John Thornton in Toronto, who works with people who've suffered brain injuries, as well as utilizing the Eight Steps of Master Mind Principle created by the late Jack Boland (a Unity Minister), I've been able to begin to pull out of this horrific experience. Will I ever be able to find real meaning and purpose in my life? I can say unequivocally that I am willing to do whatever needs to be done so that I can be really happy again and I believe from the bottom of my heart I will be able to solve both the emotional and financial issues that have arisen from this unfortunate situation.

What would transpire three years after the initial assault is that the injury I sustained damaged my ability to create new projects and close new business.

I am thankful to say that up until that point I have had an amazing career and a great deal of producing experience. Our most recent CBC Production, *Super Volcano, Yellowstone's Fury* was the highest rated production for Doc

Zone for 2013 and will play in the United States on the Smithsonian Channel in 2014. It was an idea my brother Jim suggested to me. Doc Zone is the strand that is analogous to the 'brass ring' for independent producers of documentaries in Canada and the CBC is the world's second largest public broadcaster after the BBC.

Two of my other documentaries in late 2012 and early 2013 were rated in the top three for the year. In 2011 our series *Yonge Street, Toronto Rock & Roll Stories* that aired on Bravo and CTV 2 garnered significant critical acclaim and awards. It too was also started in early 2009. In addition, our production of *The Gangster Next Door*, which aired in 2011 was also started in 2009 and was one of CBC Doc Zones' top three rated shows for that year.

I seem to be competent with the process of producing, but what I can't do, as I've noted above is 'close' new business, which is the most important part of my job and why I've had the title, producer and executive producer of over 130 episodes of prime time drama, comedies, docudramas, and documentaries and four feature films, for such studios as United Artists, Disney and Zoetrope Studios.

As a result of this experience, I got to thinking, "how many other people, especially those who are either middle aged, or those of us who are 'baby boomers', get blindsided by some event that they didn't see coming?"

Would you know what to do if you had a life altering illness, accident or totally unexpected event happen to you that you and that you had no control over? In my own case I did not.

Dr. Thornton emphasized that in addition to traditional medication I might want to examine universal spiritual principles to assist me in the healing of my injury. So employing dedication as well as the Eight Steps as the tools of transformation, I set about to heal myself and find new meaning and purpose in my life.

Please don't let the term "Master Mind Principle", throw you off. A good friend of mine pointed out that the phrase has a great deal of energy and emotion – both negative and positive assigned to it. The term was created somewhere in the early 20th century by the late great Napoleon Hill, the forerunner of the human potential movement.

In the context of this book, it is simply a way of denoting the concept of being able to access the 'Divine Intelligence of the Universe or Spark' of the 'Creator's Consciousness' or the "Master Mind" of God that we can utilize to change our lives for the better. If that word causes you any distress, then please substitute 'Divine Mind' or any other phrase that would indicate something you can believe in – whether it is simply nature or the power of the ocean if you prefer.

I want to emphasize that this book is not suggesting a religious solution per se, but rather one spiritual in nature. It's whatever you conceive to be the 'Divine Mind' or God, as you understand God to be. I am not trying to convince or convert anyone to any specific theology. But I will borrow heavily from other spiritual movements that have emerged over the last several centuries.

As I looked around I realized that there are very few guides or how-to manuals on how to handle these major life altering transitions, from either a busy active career or professional life to "how we cope with events like an unexpected illness or life changing injury, the loss of a partner, the end of a marriage, or our own eventual death."

What about the supposed "golden years"? There is absolutely no instruction booklet on how to handle the inevitable crises that are certain to arise over time. I know our banks, financial institutions and insurance companies like to talk to us about our finances, but what about family relations, business relations and life long friendships? What do we do if we find ourselves at odds with those closest to us, or our family members we've not spoken to for decades?

For those of us who are further along in life, we really do need to clean up these relationships before we die so we can have real peace of mind and real happiness in our latter years. No one wants to leave the planet in a state of discord with his or her family. However, we are all going to reach the departure lounge - one day. Will you be ready?

Most importantly, I would like to examine how we could live our lives such that we can find a way to cope, stay happy, be productive and create some purpose in life – especially if we encounter some unexpected difficulties or challenges.

These were all the questions racing through my mind in that late spring and early summer 2013.

At times I feel hopeful, other times hopeless. I have cried a lot in the last few weeks. I have felt very alone and afraid.

I may have to put my house in the country up for sale as I've gone over one year with no new projects to produce and I've slowly kept downsizing my company and burning through a lot of cash keeping the doors open and my staff employed. One by they have been leaving as they know I don't have the resources to keep going. I am really facing some very big challenges.

I want to emphasize this point. I don't wish to offend anyone with some of the information here, and I hope that you won't find what I'm about share in bad taste. It's simply what happened to me.

That said, I will strive to be rigorously honest with you as I undergo the process of coming up with a solution to my current financial, emotional and spiritual challenges as a result of my injury. If I can find a way to be of service while sharing my story and hopefully help someone and perhaps myself, then I believe we've all won. I will not shy away from describing the feelings I'm having, or the difficulties I'm going through.

One of my intentions is to use this book as a vehicle that will enable me to deliver keynote talks on overcoming adversity, finding peace of

A gift from
Leah Rasmussen

I thought I would surprise you with a gift! Rita, I thought you would enjoy this book. Love : Wayne & Leah

Have feedback on Amazon gifting? Tell us at www.amazon.com/giftingfeedback.

SDI9SC07MN

ft from
ah Rasmussen

er ID 109-6336290-6117864 - Order of October 16, 2014

Item
Aging with Dignity, Living with Grace: 8 Steps to Help You Overcome Adversity, Find Peace of Mind & Prosperity in the Se... Brady, David H. --- Paperback (** 1-B-1 **) 1621374742
Aging with Dignity, Living with Grace: 8 Steps to Help You Overcome Adversity, Find Peace of Mind & Prosperity in the Se... Brady, David H. --- Paperback (** 1-B-1 **) 1621374742

urns Are Easy! Most items can be refunded, exchanged, or replaced when returned riginal and unopened condition. Visit http://www.amazon.com/returns to start your rn, or http://www.amazon.com/help for more information on return policies.

DI9SC07MN/-2 of 2-//IPARCEL-NJ/std-intl-us-

mind and prosperity and work with corporations and sales organizations on how to create and sell big ideas.

We producers are some of the world's best sales people. We get an idea. We have to 'sell' or convince a network, studio or distributor to give us the equivalent amount of money that it would take to build an office building, an apartment building or at least a large mansion, all based on an idea or concept that I or someone else dreamed up. It is the ultimate intangible. That takes real skill.

Whether I will ever have a producing career again, is still up in the air. What I can tell you is I'm betting my life savings that I will be able to recreate myself as a university lecturer as well as a motivational/inspirational speaker and writer of non-fiction books.

I wrote in my first book, *Get Me To the Temple of Serenity . . . And Step On It!*, "we are once again, in the midst of very trying times." The late Psychiatrist, Scott Peck, who wrote *The Road Less Traveled* said, "Life is difficult". It was so for him, and in spite of all his medical and empirical knowledge, he left this planet a broken man. According to those close to him he was an unrecovered alcoholic with many unresolved relationship issues.

If the last thing you ever imagined is that you would be facing a health issue, financial challenges, your business closing unexpectedly, a family, friendship, or marriage difficulty, or God forbid, the loss of a loved one, then welcome to the club. You are no longer alone.

–HOW TO READ THIS BOOK–

I have been using the Eight Steps of the Master Mind Principle myself with great success for over a dozen years.

The first thing I want to share with you is that I have not written this book as a traditional self help publication. I am going to utilize the Eight Step Principles to help you the reader overcome whatever adversity it is you are facing, find peace of mind and prosperity. My style of writing is also more conversational than a formal behavioural science tome.

In Part One, I am going to take you on a road trip back in time. It will be part biographical and part philosophical. I believe it is important for you the reader to know my experience.

In Part Two, I'm going to use my daily journal as the framework, to allow the events to unfold as they are happening to me, in real time, beginning the first week of July, 2013 and ending where I am today, February 18, 2014.

Those journal sections will have the text inside of a box. At the same time, I will introduce the Eight Steps of the Master Mind Principle and draw on my interdisciplinary background in working these steps in all areas of my life. I will use my own journey as the backbone of Part Two, and how it is I am applying the steps to overcome the difficulties I'm facing.

What I can say today with certainty is that the circumstances of my life have already changed for the better as a result of employing these steps.

If you just want help or are in a crisis, then please feel free to proceed immediately to Part Two. I won't be offended.

–CONTENTS–

–Part One–
  –Chapter One–
    Let Me Introduce Myself 1
  –Chapter Two–
    My, Generation 13
  –Chapter Three–
    Time Flies When You are Having Fun! 26

–Part Two–
  –Chapter Four–
    There is a Solution 33
  –Chapter Five–
    How To Work The Steps:
    I Surrender 37
  –Chapter Six–
    I Believe 48
  –Chapter Seven–
    I Am Ready To Be Changed 59
  –Chapter Nine–
    I Decide to be Changed 70
  –Chapter Nine–
    I Forgive 96
  –Chapter Ten–
    I Ask 109
  –Chapter Eleven–
    I Give Thanks 128
  –Chapter Twelve–
    I Dedicate My Life 137

-Part One-

-Chapter One-

Let Me Introduce Myself

On the next page is a picture of me in Toronto in the summer of 1964. I was 16 years old. I want to let you know where I came from and what I've learned during my lifetime. This will give you a sense of who I am today, and why you might be interested in what I have to say. If I were you, I would certainly want to know, who is this man and why should I pay any attention to him? While I have outlined some of my recent success in the foreword, just what qualifies me to write a self help book, you may be asking? After all, you may be a captain of industry, a lawyer, physician, engineer, housewife, banker, politician or an everyday working woman or man.

To answer the above mentioned question, let us go back and start in the 1960s. If you can remember them, you weren't there according to my friends. To start with, I was part of the live hard, die young and leave a good-looking corpse philosophy that was based on ignorance of facts and inaccurate data. I was so naïve back then. In truth I was raised in a very privileged background.

At 16, I was a rebel and I drove a motorcycle. Was I dangerous? Not in my private school blazer, or my button down white shirt and my Bass Weejun penny loafers. I rode a BSA 650 and I loved the speed and the freedom that motorcycle gave me. And I was the first young man at my private school that drove one. The compression was high on it, and I was so skinny back then I used to have to run down the street and jump on it in second gear to get it started (no electric start of course and a kick start that kicked back and fired me over the handle bars once). It had straight pipes, no front fender and the license plate was sitting off the back lock nut holding the wheel on. It looked cool.

As I look back at that photograph today, I just smile. But here is what I was like. I would start drinking with a small group of my likeminded friends. I would end up on that motorcycle in Toronto, where I lived. Most of my friends grew up in Rosedale or Moore Park in Toronto. My mother and I were in Deer Park, the area just north of St. Clair that ran between Yonge Street on the east and Avenue Road on the west. These were nice neighborhoods. I would arrive at a young lady's house, park the BSA out front and stroll up to the door feeling like Peter Fonda on steroids.

Now, when I wasn't drinking, I was so shy it was hard to get a word out of me. But, after imbibing a few, my mind said that I could give Don Juan a run for his money. On a few occasions, the mothers would say, "David, my daughter is not going out with you on that machine!" I'd sort of lean up against the door just like I'd seen Jean Paul Belmondo do in the French New Wave cinema that was the rage at the time and say, "What are you doing? Want to come for a ride?" They didn't all slam the door in my face. I was bad. But it was fun. At least a few times, I was very pleasantly surprised. Hello Mrs. Robinson.

Honest to God, as I think of it now, and being a parent with four of my own kids (and two daughters) and four grandkids, I just think back on those days, shake my head and smile. I really was so innocent. I also say a prayer: "Please forgive me for all the crazy things I did, but please never let me forget how enjoyable it was."

I want to state for the record that I was a disaster as a student back then. I always quit high school near the end of the year so I wouldn't fail.

I never opened a book, except once. I was at a private cram school, Meisterchaft College, right behind my former prep school, De La Salle Oaklands, on Woodlawn Avenue.

To the best of my memory, I was writing a grade 12 Geography exam. The night before I thought, "I'd better at least look at the text book."

My poor mother was paying several thousand dollars a year in 1967 for me to attend this private school for teenagers like me who had a lot of "learning issues". Like never showing up. I was drunk most days after lunch at the Embassy Tavern or the Place Pigalle on Avenue Road. Then I would be obnoxious to the teachers. To the outside world we appeared rich and spoiled (which in my case was not as my Mom made an astounding sacrifice for me to attend). That said, the teachers were actually very good.

I sort of found the book interesting and stayed up reading it. It actually had my attention. The only other subject I enjoyed this much had been English history. Canadian History bored me to death.

The next morning I wrote the exam and the following day, the teacher, Jay asked me to stay after school. When I arrived, he sat me down. "Whom did you cheat from?" he asked. I looked at him and said, "What are you talking about?" He smiled oddly, as if he'd caught me dead in my tracks. "You have the highest mark in the class. I know you've never even come close to a mark like this before." I smiled right back at him and with real confidence said, "I read the book."

I can still remember the look on his face of total disbelief. "Oh yeah, would you sit here right now and write it again?" As best as I can remember, I smiled, "Sure, but if I ace it I want you to lend me your Corvette." He had the sweetest 1964 or 65 green Stingray.

This actually happened. He said something like, "You bet." I sat down and rewrote the exam and scored even higher. He was dumfounded. That started a friendship with this teacher where he and I would go out drinking after school, and I would tell him about our Rock & Roll business, which stunned him even more. He couldn't believe what my friend John Brower and I were doing. And he lent me the Corvette.

My Early Career

At this time, my brother Jim got me a job on the floor of the Toronto Stock Exchange. It was there that I would get my fundamental lesson in economics.

I loved working on the floor as it was called, first as a post boy, marking the various stock prices that were *bid* and *asked* from the various brokers who would yell at me to change the prices, and then as a phone clerk for a brokerage firm.

During this same period, my oldest friend, John Brower, who appeared in our recent television production of *Yonge Street, Toronto Rock & Roll Stories*, began talking about our getting serious about starting up a record company.

In the summer of 1967, John Brower, Bob McBride, who would go on to sing with the band Lighthouse (*Sunny Days, One Fine Morning*) and I boarded an American Airlines flight to Los Angeles. That was the beginning of the career that I've carried on with to this day, with stops along the way to educate myself.

During that summer in Los Angeles, my life changed totally. It was as a result of that experience, and then coming back to Toronto, that I realized I couldn't safely drink alcohol and so in March 1970, at the age of 22, I stopped drinking. I have never had another drink to this day, forty-four years.

At 21, I found myself working on the floor of the Toronto Stock Exchange at a Montreal brokerage firm, Bouchard and Company. Once again, through my brother Jim, I would meet my second oldest best friend that I still have today, Mike O'Shea, who was my immediate supervisor. Those were the days when I'd go out for lunch, have about six quick drinks in a row, and then go back and start taking orders from Mike for the Pro Trader, Bobby Dunbar. I was just the guy you wanted to help execute your trading orders. Somehow, though, I always managed to pull it off.

I was married for the first time at the age of 21. That marriage only lasted a few years. It was at this time that I utilized my experience of working in the brokerage business and went to work as a financial planner. I spent three years with two major Canadian insurance companies before my manager and I formed ASK Corporation. We sought out the advice of Bob Proctor, who was early in his career in the human potential movement. Through him, my manager and I ended up with purchasing one of the Earl Nightingale Distributorships, which allowed us to get into the business of motivating and inspiring both individuals and corporations through Earl's audio programs. It was through this that I acquired my early experience in public speaking.

I'm grateful to say that my first marriage produced my two oldest children Andrew and Colleen. They are both married today and have children of their own, and it's been a wonderful experience reconnecting with them. Andrew had the opportunity to work with me when he came out of university, and I just emailed my daughter Colleen about driving down with her mom later on this month to visit her, her husband Rob and two of my grandkids, Guerin and Conlan. She is in Franklin, near Nashville Tennessee. I am so proud of all my kids.

Higher Education

When that marriage ended, I made the decision to return to school and went to Humber College in Toronto to study journalism. I'd always wanted to be a writer.

After two years, I transferred to Simon Fraser University in Burnaby, British Columbia. That is the only decision I've ever made that I've regretted as it took me out of Andrew and Colleen's life for almost fifteen years, except for the occasional visit. I was studying Communications - not film and television - but the behavioural sciences: Gregory Bateson, Systems Theory, and working toward becoming an Alcohol and Drug Counselor.

My Introduction to Filmmaking

After my undergraduate studies, I was admitted to Graduate School at SFU. It was there that I made my first film, *Alcohol, Drugs and the Young in British Columbia,* with the Royal Canadian Mounted Police in North Vancouver.

I received an A for that film and thought, "Hmm, sit in an office and listen to people go on about life, or travel around the world, meet interesting people and have a whole lot of fun making films." It took about a nanosecond to make that choice.

During this time I also began my first teaching assignment working as a Teaching Assistant for the Chair of the department, Bill Melody, and his long time friend and associate, Dallas Smythe. They were both Political Economists.

After I made the decision to leave the track of training to be a therapist, I met and began producing movies with my late business partner, Phillip Borsos. Those years were remarkable and out of them would come tremendous critical success. In 1980, I accompanied Phillip to the Academy Awards as a result of his nomination for *Nails*. By now I owned 40% of Phil's company and had helped finance the finishing of *Nails*.

Less than two years later we would be launched onto the world stage with *The Grey Fox*, which was nominated for two Golden Globe Awards, Best Foreign Picture and Best Actor for Richard Farnsworth. Francis Ford Coppola's Zoetrope Studios and United Artists Classics presented the film. In between I had also executive produced a small feature, *Till Death Do Us Part*, to very positive reviews in the U.S. trades and the Canadian press.

What I'm grateful to say is that I have really had an amazing life as a result of that decision. When I hear people say, "Oh, I wish I'd tried that," I can honestly say, "Not me". I did! And, it did not always end well, mind you.

It was an amazing experience the morning it was announced that the film had been nominated for two Golden Globe Awards. It is also the only film that Roger Ebert ever reviewed twice.

We would end up winning seven Genies that same year (Canadian Academy Awards) and be recognized by the international press for producing what would become one of the most critically acclaimed movies in the history of Canada. The Government of Canada made a commemorative stamp of it.

Peter O'Brian and Phil had arranged for the film to be distributed through Zoetrope Studios and Fred Roos, who was Coppola's producer, and a woman in Toronto, Linda Beath, who were able to get us a deal with United Artists Classics. Those were heady years.

Crash and Burn

About two years later, I would experience the first major reversal of my life on a feature film I was producing in Washington State.

We paid twenty five thousand dollars for financing to a law firm in New York City. They said they had four million dollars on deposit, and they would advance the funds once we paid the above-mentioned standby fee. We paid their fee and the funds never materialized. We were the victims of commercial fraud. I would end up owing over $5 million dollars Canadian, most of which has now been repaid. I did not go bankrupt as I felt I would never learn what I needed to learn if I did that.

That experience propelled me to finally get honest with myself and take one hundred percent responsibility for the fact I'd made the decision to move ahead with a project that would have been better off being left alone.

Once again, this would end up being the greatest learning experience I had ever had and my life was changed for the better. Mind you, I couldn't see it at that moment. All I could see was the mountain of debt I had and the number of people I'd hurt.

The reason I added 'middle age' to this book is because it was that experience, literally at the threshold of middle age, that would propel me toward the most productive, peace-filled and yet ironically, challenging times I ever had. Back then I was working toward reestablishing my career. My wife and I were raising two young children and acquiring a nice home in Deer Park, a lovely neighborhood in Toronto. We were educating our youngest children, and I was reestablishing my relationship with my two older children from my first marriage who were now young adults.

My Introduction to Pedagogy

It was during this period that I began my teaching career. My first faculty position was at York University in Toronto. After four or five years, I moved to Ryerson University in downtown Toronto, where I am grateful to say I won the CESAR Teaching Award. What I learned at those two institutions is that I had a real gift for teaching and communicating. Ironically, if I hadn't had the problems on the previously mentioned production, I would never have undertaken either one of those positions. I realize today what a wonderful gift teaching is, and I hope to do it again.

While teaching, I also was the founder of three production companies that all ended up being very successful and either merging with other companies or as in the case of David Brady Productions, it still in existence today but on hiatus until I can find out what the long term prognosis is for my injury.

However, in the past twenty-seven years I have written, produced or directed over one hundred and thirty episodes of prime time television along with four feature films. I can't even begin to list the awards we've either been nominated for or won.

Generally, my life has, in spite of the occasional speed bump brought on by indecision, impatience, self-centeredness, anger or fear – fear that I would not get what I wanted or lose what I had – been remarkable. It has been filled with so many wonderful events and people that I just sit here amazed at where I've been and whom I've met.

While I do have a few regrets, they are not many. What I have is a rich treasure trove of memories and accomplishments and an outstanding cadre of family, friends and associates with whom I've spent my entire life.

–Chapter Two–

My, Generation

People try to put us d-down (Talkin' 'bout my generation) The Who

If you were born between 1945 and 1965 you will remember the refrain, "Don't trust anyone over thirty." We were the generation that created that myth, and we are the generation that can change it. Conversely, if we were operating out of the flawed paradigm from that day and applying it to our lives today, we'd say, "Don't trust anyone under fifty". I really believe now that nothing could be further from the truth.

I am so happy to say that my children are so much more responsible than we were. I'd like to be like them when I grow up.

The bill of goods we sold ourselves about youth being the only way, the better way, the enlightened way, that being groovy and hip, was flawed. However, many of the principles of our youth were sound. Make love, not war, (just not to so many people ... it's not good for you or anyone else for that matter). Social justice, right on. Reconciling with our First Nations citizens is vital to the health of our country.

My Take on Neurobiology

Finding an answer to war - what do we need to do to realize we are operating out of a part of our brain that is millions of years old will never work? Violence will never solve any problem, and yet it is often the first avenue that we pursue. It is hard wired into our brains. Our reptilian/mammalian brain is connected that way to save us from aggressive predators. The only trouble is that there are no more dinosaurs on the planet. But you can't tell that to our brainstem. According to Dr. Paul MacLean, the triune brainstem is responsible for aggression, territorial and reproductive behaviour. They are the primary triggers for all of our problems in life.

While it was helpful for our survival, hundreds of thousands, or even millions of years ago, it ends up causing us untold grief, regret and pain when we let it control our body and minds. It will have us say and do things that, when we are not in our "right mind", we should never say or do. Essentially we have outdated software in our brains. That is why we need to utilize tools like the Eight Steps, to reprogram our thinking so we can overcome these ancient triggers that create so many problems for us.

My Take on Sociology

Society's worshipping at the altar of youth has ended up creating a massive schism that is both counter-intuitive and counter-productive. Ironically, what some advertisers thought was a dream come true in the 18 to 35 year old demographic has proven to be less than perfect. As it turns out, according to some economists, it is our aging population, including the 'baby boomer' that is controlling the purse strings of the world's economy and we are in charge of over eighty percent of wealth on the planet today.

We still have a voracious appetite for spending and consuming, on either quality projects like philanthropy or art and culture, or consumer goods like cars, motorcycles, motor homes, vacation homes, travel, food, alcohol and gifts for those we love. But are the latter the only things we should be pursuing? If we believe they are the key to our happiness, then I believe those beliefs should be analyzed.

How happy are you with your Mercedes Benz, BMW or Lexus, a beach-house in California, a condo in Florida or a home in the Hamptons? I want to point out that there is nothing wrong with any of those items if you are also using your resources to make a difference in the world. I have a Mercedes myself.

EGO
(Edge Good Or God Out)

However if all you are doing is satisfying an insatiable urge to have more in order to appease your ego, then I suspect you are not a happy camper. The question I would ask is what have you done lately to make a difference on the planet if you are fortunate enough to be in a position to help others?

I recently had lunch with a woman, Pamela Bendall, who is a 'boomer' and in her previous life was a very successful stockbroker. She has just written her own book, *"What Was I Thinking?"* It is a must read. She describes her dream of building her own 56-foot sailboat 'Precious Metal' and sailing singlehandedly from British Columbia down to the South Pacific. That took incredible skill, courage and a sense of self that most people will never find.

Did she just sail for her own gratification? No, and as a result of her travels, she has started up schools in Mexico and is now educating over seven thousand children. The UN have decided to make her organization the example of what an individual can do this coming year, which will be the Year of Education.

Have you, like me found that those material pursuits alone are very short-lived one-way love affairs? They only supply us with a very temporary sense of satisfaction and little or no peace of mind. I have. I remember getting the new Chrysler 300 the year after they were rereleased in 2006. I wasn't off the lot and down the street a few miles when my mind started up. Why didn't you get the 300 C? I like that metallic grey one. Why did I get a black one?

And what about those of us who haven't planned for our futures as well as we should have? What will happen to us? Once again my mind starts up. "You will end up penniless, a pauper working a corner with a cup!"

This needn't happen if we keep our wits about us. Youth is fine for backbreaking and heavy slugging but, the intellect of those who are more mature, gifted with our wealth of experience, is worth its weight in gold. And we can all realize this with some simple steps and planning.

If you can remember back when life was "groovy", we didn't have a care in the world. That is a great place to get back to. And it's attainable. How? By simply following the recipe, I'm going to lay out in part two of this book and the later chapters with the Eight Steps of the Master Mind. Did we have a lot of money? No, probably not. But, we likely had friends and fun.

What's the truth about being young? Our bodies are supple. We have higher sex drives. We can take falls and brushes with death more easily. We have more energy. We have great expectations. We have wonderful plans, and we have a lot of living to look forward to. And we think we are immortal.

The Truth About Being a Baby Boomer and Aging

What is the truth about being a 'boomer', being a Sage? Many of us still have a good sex drive. It is however, much more emotional and psychological than physical. In many cases, it is based on true intimacy rather than raw, self-centered sexual satisfaction.

We do our best to avoid falls and brushes with death through an acquired wisdom and experience. We can still have wonderful expectations, and we can head out and try novel things with a new confidence – our lives won't end if we fail. We can still ski, ride motorcycles and bikes, take hikes, travel, and go on road trips and visit places we've always wanted to.

We can try new adventures or new occupations where we don't have to feel shame or blame if we don't bat a thousand. There is a wonderful book by Paul Kurtz entitled *The Spirituality of Imperfection.* In it, Kurtz points out that in baseball if you hit three hundred, you will be paid millions of dollars to join a major league baseball team. What that means is that 7 out of 10 times you will miss hitting the ball. Baseball is the only game in the world that recognizes errors as part of the process. We want to liberate ourselves from old beliefs, old self defeating thinking that we acquired somewhere between the ages of 3 and 12. None of us are perfect, and every one of us makes mistakes – and that includes you and me!

So many of us have unresolved issues from our pasts and our childhoods. It is imperative that we let go of old, self-defeating thinking about our dreams or ideas that we had in our youth that no longer support us. It is important to age gracefully.

Holding onto the idea that I need to be liked by everyone is self-defeating. Not everyone will like us. As a matter of fact, I like to say that what others think of me is none of my business. It's more important to like ourselves, just the way we are and not worry about what others think of us, period. In the majority of cases, anyone over 50 has a tad of flab. Can we look at ourselves in the mirror and say, "I love you just as you are, balding, chubby and wrinkled?" If not, here is an area that we need to examine.

Do I personally have complete freedom from this? I do not. I still glance sideways in the mirror, hold in my stomach and puff my chest up. Once again, there is that old reptilian brainstem firing up. Today, I try to thank my brainstem and mind for sharing and then give it permission to take the day off.

Our youthful years were a wonderful time. So is aging. It is one of the great treasures that many do not get to enjoy. Is it filled with challenges? Yes. Our loved ones get sick and die. Our friends move away. Other friends change and go from outgoing positive people to reclusive, angry and lonely folks that slowly withdraw from life. All we can do is wish them well and bless them. We do get lonely. We do sometimes think, "What's the point of all this?"

For many of us, it is often hard to accept that not only are we getting older, we are now in our "mature" years. There's that word again. Mature. There are some of us who've had unhappy childhoods; unfortunately they've lasted fifty or sixty years. The good news is it's never too late to have a happy childhood!

I don't know about you, but I don't feel old. I can still do everything I did at 20, or 30, or 40. I can ski, swim (which I try and do at least twice a week), and I can hike up the side of mountains in Northern California on logging roads. I have to stop occasionally, but so do 40 year-olds. I can still dance, (I don't know about the Watusi). I can still make love without needing a little pill (although I just tried one and they're fabulous).

However, we are mature (hopefully) adults who should strive to be role models of how it is to age gracefully with purpose. To try and act like a teenager, or dress in the current style of young adults is playing a form of emotional and psychological Russian roulette.

Realizing that I no longer have the body I had at 25, 35, 45 or 55, I don't think it's a good idea to take hormone replacement or some extreme form of exercise to try and emulate someone half my age. My gut instinct is it is a tragedy waiting to happen.

If it is something prescribed by a physician for health reasons that is a different story. I was stunned to find out that the medical license I paid fifty bucks for online wasn't valid. So, I'm out of the medical advice-dispensing business.

I am not talking about physical fitness either. We all should pursue that. I try to do aqua fit classes at least two days a week, but three is optimal. I also do 40 push-ups off my bathtub side three mornings a week. I walk everywhere I can. I make a point of leaving my car at home if I can. So exercise is good. Trying to emulate the Y generation? Not so much.

I believe we must have the self-confidence to be able to dress, however we want. If I'm doing it to please myself and just have fun, fabulous. But If I'm desperately doing it to cling onto the illusion of youth, well, that can be embarrassing. Our job is to be happy where we are at this stage of our lives. I still love my button down shirts and penny loafers. I just wish I could fit into my private school blazer!

Faith?

Faith. I believe it is critical to our wellbeing. Again, I want to emphasize, I'm not necessarily talking about religion, although if you have a traditional faith that works for you, then you are ahead of the game. What I am talking about is a faith in something greater than *me*. I don't care if it's your local hydro provider.

I've been an agnostic a lot of my life. I had great faith when I was young and then as I studied and educated myself beyond my own level of comprehension, I lost my childhood faith. It didn't make sense to me in light of scientific and empirical evidence (or so I thought).

Look at the randomness of the planet. Who can understand why such natural disasters as the horrific earthquake and the Indian Ocean tsunami that killed over 240,000 people in 13 countries on December 26, 2004 needed to happen if there is a loving Supreme Being?

Then there is the insanity of the shootings in Sandy Hook Elementary School. What about the fact that the Nazis killed six million Jews and others during the Second World War in Concentration Camps?

Joseph Stalin killed close to thirty million of his own citizens. I'm sure they all believed in God and prayed for help. But, where was God in these times? It makes me wonder, as portrayed in the wonderful Hollywood film that many critics consider the best film of all time – *Casablanca*, when Humphrey Bogart's Rick says to Ingrid Bergman's character, "I've got a job to do, too. Where I'm going, you can't follow. What I've got to do, you can't be any part of Ilsa. I'm no good at being noble, but it doesn't take much to see that the problems of three little people don't amount to a hill of beans in this crazy world. Someday you'll understand that."

And it is true that our problems won't amount to a hill of beans, except to us. Who can remember what they were worried about ten years ago, five years ago, six months ago? I can guarantee you, at the time it was such a crisis you never thought you would find a solution.

As a result of those horrible circumstances, you may have thought that your life was over. But now you can hardly remember what it was that was so bad. I exclude experiencing the death of a loved one, being seriously ill, being cheated on by a partner, or losing a business from this situation. Those hurts cut deep and to the bone and take both time and psychological or spiritual assistance to heal.

So how do we reconcile a Divine Being who allows these horrific events to transpire but is supposedly filled with love for all humanity? I think that Rabbi Harold Kushner in his groundbreaking book, *When Bad Things Happen to Good People* does a much better job of explaining it than I can.

But here is what I believe. These unexplained horrific events are some of the great paradoxical mysteries of life. And one I don't think I will get a real answer to anytime soon. It is only when we shuffle off this mortal coil and then find ourselves either in a very deep slumber for all eternity, or, present in the radiance of a supreme being whom I'm willing to bet will not be standing there with a clipboard, a scowl on His/Her/Its face saying either verbally or telepathically, " Hi Dave, I've been expecting you". Then, a large trap door opens and I find myself being hurled into the endless pit of fire.

Alas, that's how my childhood Roman Catholic mind works. Talk about insanity. And that's after the Catholic Church cancelled Hell as a geographic location. But it is so deeply ingrained in my unconscious that it is the first place my mind goes whenever I find myself in my normal state of being a human being who makes mistakes.

What kind of God would create a species, then fry their derriere off for being exactly the way they were made; imperfect in every way. Flawed emotions, flawed values, flawed instincts that run wild (lust, jealousy, rage, greed), and flawed physiology that wears out and dies.

Or, is it that there is a rhythm to life that always ends in a transformative stage at death? (Or, at least what we call death). What if it is simply a gateway to another reality, another dimension that is parallel to this one?

Today there are a growing number of quantum physicists who believe this is the case, and they estimate they are only a decade or two away from discovering its mystery. What is the common thread here? It is all the information that is coming into my brain and being processed by my limbic system – and it is part of the old brainstem. So, while the brain has added new hemispheres in the neo-cortex and the temporal lobes that actually are responsible for our wondering about God, it's the old reptilian guy/gal up there, running the show. Time to let him/her go.

Acceptance: a very wise man, who was a doctor and an alcoholic once said (and I paraphrase), "Acceptance is the key to all of our problems in life." When we rail against time, the fact we have aged, when we rail against the injustices of the monetary system, the (supposed) free markets that we embrace, the people whom we perceive have harmed us, the government, our ex husbands, or wives we cannot find peace of mind or happiness. Whatever it is we are not happy with, it is our problem, not the other person's.

We don't accept injustice either. But, we need to be prudent in how we find a solution.

We don't get out of our automobiles and confront an erratic driver who may be impaired and dangerous. We call 911 in North America, or whatever the number is in the country in which you are reading this and allow our law enforcement agencies to handle the situation. Trying to take the law into our own hands is actually dangerous and can lead to tragic events as was witnessed with the horrible murder of the young Trayvon Martin in Florida in 2012.

When it comes to families, many of us have had situations where family members had difficulty communicating appropriately because of anger or fear. They say and do things that are not acceptable. For many of us, we had to seek outside help to overcome the challenges of living in a dysfunctional family situations created by alcohol, drugs, anger, or abandonment issues. It is important to remember that many of these people are suffering from a disease.

So, acceptance of their condition is important, but it is also never appropriate to accept their behaviour when they are being abusive

–Chapter Three–

Time Flies When You are Having Fun!

So, there I was minding my own business at age 39, in a second marriage with two young children. I had just lost a lot of money on a movie I was producing, and I calculated I had a good 25 to 30 years to make a comeback. No problem. Relaxed, I went to bed and woke up at age 65.

I was stunned. How could this be? I wish I'd planned better. But the time between 39 and 65 flew by like a rocket. You might say that it was like riding the head of a ballistic missile, unguided, as it would turn out. When I stop and take stock, here is where I am. I have a nice home in the country, mostly paid for, and a nice apartment in Toronto. I have a reasonable amount of savings. I'm still running my production company at least for the next week. Earlier this year, I had the highest rated show for a major network here in Canada.

What I had was the talent and ability to conceive an idea and translate that onto the screen so that significant numbers of people would want to watch what we created and produced.

More importantly, in the past, when I made 10 pitches, I would end up with between 1 and 3 productions on average. Now I'm not connecting on any of these projects.

My last four productions were started before the assault, except for one, which my brother Jim gave me. That was the *Yellowstone Super Volcano* production. My youngest son Brendan and Anthony, who work with me, came up with our two previous Vision Productions.

Cindy Banks who was the catalyst for *The Real Girls of New York City* may also save us with this idea.

We're sitting here on pins and needles waiting for word. Will we be able to stay in business, or will I have to figure out what the next stage of my life is and how I will survive and manage to live a life of quality and self-respect?

What are my choices? I can now focus on a new career writing and speaking. I can see if I can be hired to a teaching position. I'd like to. I have won a teaching award, so I know I have that ability.

Ironically, it is the golden age of television drama on the US and Canadian cable networks.

I will need to make a decision. And so will you, if you are about to embark on any major changes in your life due to a financial setback, the loss of a job or management position, or if you are one of us boomers who are fortunate enough to be retiring. You may be impacted by the financial meltdown that occurred after

2008. You may have experienced the loss of your spouse or life partner, or your closest friends. You may have been recently diagnosed with a life altering illness, whether it's terminal or not.

I think it's important for any of us, whether self-employed or as an executive or manager, or as a frontline employee, to do an inventory of our assets. That inventory should include not only our financial assets, but also our family, friends, health, mementos of our past, keepsakes from our children, awards, and a list our achievements.

It really is a very good idea to do this. It is also important to sit down and look at every aspect of your finances too.

Why? Because the same brain that lies to us, will also try to convince us that are completely deficient. My mind will tell me "I don't really have all the skills necessary to proceed with something that is out of my comfort zone". It might say, "You've worked at Acme Tool and Gear all of your life, and now you want to start up a bookstore cafe. How crazy is that?" Not very if you are innovative and add things like coffee, comfortable chairs, author's readings, a gift shop, book club and make it a centre for the community. This is just an example.

Earlier in this process I signed up with Jack Canfield Coaching because I couldn't close deals. I am committed to healing myself and moving forward, and I am trying to do everything within my power to mitigate this situation.

And while the coaching may not solve that specific problem, it has already brought to light this very point. I have had a lot of success in my life, which my brain has conveniently forgotten, and thus my mind tells me "loser". Once again, I must say to my mind, "thank you for sharing and you can have the rest of the day off."

Here is what is ironic about my occupation. I was always yelled at as a child in school for daydreaming. Here I am a lifetime later, and I've been paid enormously well to sit around and dream up ideas. Again, as I said, my body of work is fairly extensive.

Here's the thing. I get an idea, and I go and sit in meetings with Executives at studios or networks and say, "Here we go." And off I go explaining a concept. Then, on average, 3 out of 10 times (batting 300) they say, "Okay, we like it." And then we sit down and negotiate for months on end and finally the day comes when a contract arrives for an amount in the millions of dollars, all based on an idea that we've come up with.

That is a rare gift, a real creative gift that I had. However, as I said, I've hit a wall. I've finished four productions in the last two years including an award winning series. Then, it all just came to an abrupt end after the physical assault.

But, instead of giving up and admitting defeat, I am committed to moving forward. And there is plenty of help if you want it. You just have to look for it.

You Are Not Alone

Thankfully, I believe my story, while different in the sense that most people don't get assaulted, is similar to that of many people out there whose lives have been altered because of a serious car accident or industrial accident, the loss of their marriage, the death of a partner or the financial meltdown over the past five or six years.

Here is the good news. If I can find a way out, so can you. And here is the key: you are not to blame. You may have to take responsibility for what's happened to you and not get caught up in a victim stance, but you don't have to give up.

I may also have to change course in my life. For any of you who are sailors, you know that frequently we have to tack when we're heading into the wind and go in another direction to get to where we are going.

At times, it will appear we are going the wrong way as we go from a starboard tack to a port tack. And I may have to be ready to let go of old ideas in the event that there is something new trying to make its way into my life.

There are countless millions of others out there going through the same thing that you and I are. The key is to find fellow travelers with whom you can share your journey in a safe environment and thus overcome whatever adversity life throws at you.

We deserve to enjoy the benefits of our hard work in these 'golden years' in a way our parents or grandparents could never have ever imagined. "We are the Champions" as Freddy Mercury, sang in his iconic hit song with his band Queen, back in the 70s.

So, how you ended up here was by showing up and not dying. From the point at age thirty-five until today seems like it's only been a few years. Yet, it's been thirty. To many people, it's half a lifetime. It's gone by so quickly. So, what I have accomplished?

Taking Stock of Our Lives

The one thing that Jack Canfield's coaching did was make me aware of a very important fact. One of our exercises was to create an inventory of my successes. And I have had many more successes than failures. But at that time, my mind was saying, "All you've done is fail." I don't know about you, but I have a mind that lies to me. It has a 'faulty filter'.

So what is the truth? Yes, I've had disappointments. Who hasn't? But as a result of taking responsibility for them and doing the work that needed to be done, I've been able to clean up the wreckage of my past. Financially I've probably paid back eighty, or ninety per cent of the people I harmed through indebtedness. And, more importantly I've never had any of those kinds of financial problems again.

In addition was able to make amends to my first family. Today, I have a wonderful and healthy connection with my two children,

Andrew and Colleen and my ex wife Bev. I'm pleased to say we have four amazing grandkids, Sophie, Guerin, Henry and Conan.

I was married a second time to a very funny lady, Deborah, and as a result of that union, we have two children who are now young adults, Brendan and Laurel. They have both worked with me in the past.

What else have I been able to do? I was able to teach as a faculty member of two universities, York University and Ryerson University in Toronto, where I was the recipient of the CESAR teaching award.

In addition to my film and television productions, I've been President of several film and television production companies that have enjoyed tremendous critical and financial success.

I have also had the privilege of working with a lot of people over the years in a number of disciplines, and I've had the pleasure of meeting some of the most intelligent, noteworthy and influential people on the planet. So there is hope. And I sincerely hope that I am not being too arrogant to suggest as I did in the opening that I may have something to share that could be of value to you.

–Part Two–

–Chapter Four–

There is a Solution

And the solution is the Eight Steps of Master Mind Principles. I've outlined my own life succinctly (I hope) and just so you know, I'm there with you too. I'm not making this up. What are the Eight Steps created by Jack Boland?

Eight Steps Into the Master Mind Principles

1. I SURRENDER
I admit that, of myself, I am powerless to solve my problems, powerless to improve my life. I need help.

2. I BELIEVE
I now come to believe that a power great than myself --- The Infinite Creative Intelligence - the Master Mind can change my life.

3. I AM READY TO BE CHANGED
I realize that erroneous self-defeating thinking is the cause of my problems, unhappiness, fears and failures. I am ready to be changed so my life can be transformed.

4. I DECIDE TO BE CHANGED
I make a decision to surrender my will and my life to the Master Mind. I ask to be changed at depth.

5. I FORGIVE
I forgive myself for all my mistakes and shortcomings. I also forgive all other persons who may have harmed me.

6. I ASK
I make known my specific requests, asking my partner's support in knowing that the Master Mind is fulfilling my needs. (Make your request now: "I request ____"

GROUP RESPONSE: "I know the Master Mind has heard you and is providing you with what you have asked for."

7. I GIVE THANKS
I give thanks that the Master Mind is responding to my needs and I assume the same feelings I would have if my requests were fulfilled.

8. I DEDICATE MY LIFE
I now have a covenant in which it is agreed that the Master Mind is supplying me with an abundance of all things necessary to live a successful and happy life.

I dedicate myself to be of maximum service to God and those around me; to live in a manner that sets the highest example for others to follow, and to remain responsive to God's direction.

I go forth with a spirit of enthusiasm, excitement and expectancy.

I am at peace.

Adapted from Jack Boland's work at Renaissance Unity. Copyright 2005

Setting up a Master Mind Group

How does this work? First and foremost, check online sites that will allow all readers to hook up with other likeminded folks so you will not be alone. I'd recommend that a group be set up at your church, synagogue, temple or fellowship. It doesn't matter what religion you are, or, if you even have a religion. This is God, as you understand God to be. God can be an acronym for Good Orderly Direction.

It is suggested that you have no more than 6 to 8 people in your group. Everyone needs the opportunity to share and be prayed for. For many people, the idea of having their wishes affirmed is totally foreign and really uncomfortable as it takes a level of trust that many people have never experienced. There are ways around this.

If you don't belong to a church, synagogue, temple or fellowship and you are living alone or in a retirement residence, you can go online and look up information on how to form a group. As I indicated earlier, the original principles of the Master Mind were created by Napoleon Hill early in the twentieth century if you want to Google it. Regardless of their age, the principles are as true today as they were when he revolutionized the business world by creating a new paradigm for success. In fact, Napoleon Hill is the forerunner of all the people today such as Jack Canfield and Dr. Wayne Dyer, who write inspirational material, to name just a few. His insights and wisdom are timeless.

How do the steps work? I know from experience that they've worked wonders in my life. But today, the circumstances of my life are completely changed. It is my intention to be as forthright and open as I can. I want to share my journey of implementing the Eight Steps as I pursue a spiritual, emotional, as well as financial solution to my problems that will create real peace of mind.

Unity Churches across North America do have established Master Mind Groups and you can check with them too.

–Chapter Five–

How To Work The Steps:

I Surrender

STEP 1. I SURRENDER
I admit that, of myself, I am powerless to solve my problems, powerless to improve my life. I need help.

Are these steps the only way to solve your problems? Absolutely not! In some cases, you may need to seek professional help from financial advisors, insurance companies, banks, doctors lawyers, accountants, social workers, therapists, psychologists, psychiatrists and other health care practitioners. I'm not suggesting for one moment we will have all the answers in these steps.

However, I can guarantee you that your life will improve if you practice these to the best of your ability and find a way to connect to a Master Mind group of your own, either in person or online if you are living remotely or are unable to get out and have access to the internet.

Here is what I wrote in my journal the first week of July 2013:

I'm really at a loss to understand how it is that after all these years of recovery, all the work I've done, all the praying and meditating that I'm on the verge of losing a great deal of what I've worked for - my company, my home, my financial security.

We've now been turned down on 280 + submissions to broadcasters in Canada, The USA and UK. I've now dug into my own pocket for over a year to pay my company expenses, the rent on the apartment in Toronto and to cover all my credit cards and lines of credit.

I've put my house up for sale. I don't know what else to do God. I've prayed and asked you consistently for over a year to help me know your will. I've prayed and sought to do your will. I've paid $5,000 to Jack Canfield Coaching. While it did not produce the results I wanted, it did help.

I've written out my goals. I've submitted so many projects, and I've asked everyone I know to help me get business.

What can I do? What should I do? One of the books I'm reading says I can ask for help and trust in you. I've tried to do that from the bottom of my heart. I've tried to turn my will and life over to your care. How do I totally let go and trust? I want to do it. I am powerless and I need help.

I don't understand how you function. I don't know where there is justice – is that the right word, or fairness, or outcomes. All I know God is I would like to let go and accept that I am powerless and trust that I will totally be taken care of. Help me to trust, please

Have you ever found yourself in a situation where you just don't know what to do? Have you ever felt that life was not worth living? Maybe you've thought, time has passed me by, and now I'm worthless, or worse yet, a burden on my family, or society because of my age?

Have you thought about ending your life because the future looks hopeless and you cannot find a solution or see a way out? Are you so filled with fear and anxiety that you cannot find any semblance of peace or purpose in your life? Are you filled with rage and resentment because of someone or some institution that you feel has hurt you? Do you feel that the whole bill of goods we were sold in our younger years is a complete fallacy and a misrepresentation of the truth?

No matter how much you purchase, no matter how nice your home is, now matter how well your family turned out, are you left with an impending sense of doom or loss and you can't fill the hole inside of you that keeps you awake at night?

Does someone you love have a substance abuse issue? Is someone you are close to an alcoholic or drug addict? Is one of your children or siblings suffering from an eating disorder or sexual addiction? Are any of your children teetering on the edge of financial ruin or cataclysmic loss because of their lifestyles – either through gambling, or being out of control with unsecured debts including credit cards, lines of credit or loans? Is your marriage or partnership on the rocks? Are you facing a life threatening illness? Are you on the verge of going bankrupt personally or corporately?

I think you would be shocked to find out just how common it is to have these situations, thoughts or worries cross your mind, especially if you or your immediate family are one of the seventy per cent who aren't totally independent or financially self-sufficient, or in a position to be able to enjoy some of the things that life offers if you are independently wealthy.

But there are solutions. There are many fellow travelers who have faced and overcome these feelings of being powerless over their fears and worries, as well as maladaptive self-defeating behaviours.

The key to begin finding a solution to any of our problems is to admit that I am powerless over these conditions; including people, places or things and that I do need help. Once we do admit this we can begin the process of letting go and finding real peace of mind, true happiness and a genuine purpose in life regardless of our current circumstances. The first and most important thing that any of us must do is acknowledge there is a problem or situation with which we need help.

Denial does not just apply to people with alcohol, drugs, mental illness or other problems.

Accepting that we are powerless and that we need help opens the door to guidance and support from those whose lives would be enriched by assisting us, just as your life will be when it is your turn to help a fellow traveler on the road to a better life. Who really wants to admit defeat or acknowledge that we are in need of help? Pride is an awful flaw in most of us. It blinds us to our true self-worth. It keeps us locked into unhealthy self-defeating thinking and lonely lives because we don't want to look foolish, stupid, or like a failure. These are all subjective views of ourselves that are self-defeating. When I'm not in a great space, I am ruthless with myself. I beat myself up at times for making normal mistakes. I *should* myself into feeling less than and being shame-filled.

My Faulty Filter

One of my key defects is I that have a 'faulty filter': *I hear what isn't said, believe what isn't true and interpret what isn't meant.* I want to clarify this statement. My faulty filter applies to my own thinking, not to the reality of the events in my life, or the world out there. For instance, my faulty filter wanted me to minimize what had happened to me when I was physically assaulted. It wanted me to dismiss those events because I didn't want anyone not to like me (codependency). If I had followed through on my initial thought not to do anything, I would have potentially caused myself, and my family irreparable harm by listening to my faulty filter (mind).

That is why it was so good to have sober counsel from my friends and Master Mind partners who said, "You need to take care of yourself." My brother Jim had to scream at me to get my attention, so that I would do something about it.

My best friend in New York City who was my attorney also said, "You have to report this to the police because you may need medical attention and if you don't do it within a specific period, then you will impede your chance to make a claim. It has to be on record because brain injuries take time to manifest." How right he was.

My other good friend, who had also been my lawyer since 1982, said, "You have to do this. It's for your own good."

But I have to tell you I felt horrible going to the police to report the attack and to the courts and then to a lawyer because of course, I want to be liked, and this was such a personal situation.

I also have a faulty filter around worry. Ninety-five percent of what we worry about never comes to pass. The other five percent we bring on ourselves. Worry is praying for what you don't want.

Do you know anyone who is immune from worry? There are some who claim to be. There seem to be those who really do have all the nuero pathways, neurons and serotonin receptors working properly, but it is likely they really don't.

There are Zen Masters, Spiritual Giants and the likes of those who don't seem to worry. I wish I were one of them. I worry when I don't have anything to worry about. But that's me.

I've spent an entire lifetime trying to overcome the various elements of my life that

I'm powerless over and here is what I can say with absolute certainty: I am powerless over anything that changes my brain and thus the way I feel. So, I have to ensure that I don't consume any alcohol or drugs, unless a physician prescribes them. I might also add sweets when I'm stressed out.

My mind says I can have one sugarless ice cream cone a month in the summer. Somehow I'm reasonably okay with that one. However, that's my personality, and I'm powerless over it (truth be known, I can't have just one!) Damn I hate that. I believe it was Albert Einstein who said, "We can't solve problems by using the same kind of thinking we used when we created them."

We all need help from time to time, which can come from a variety of sources. There are many worthwhile self-help books, courses and support groups. We must avail ourselves of these assets and those groups in order to find the solutions we need that will make our lives richer, more peaceful and joyful, regardless of our financial situation.

My ability to earn a living has been dramatically impacted. As a result, I need help. But here's the thing - I'm powerless over the fact that I can't seem to do what I was able to do so successfully in the past.

What are my choices? I may have to give up producing. However, I'm grateful to say that I will go out on a high, creatively. I have a nice house in the country. It is an asset. I have disability insurance so I will have to see what that entails. I will have to revisit what my priorities are. .

Mental illness is a horrible affliction. I've had my own issues in my life, but never those kinds of gut-wrenching, emotional mine field that mental illness brings on.

As I said earlier, I had to quit drinking at 22, and I've never had a drink since. What I can say is that I had severe emotional issues that manifested themselves in my drinking, but my drinking and drug use was but a symptom.

Ironically that was the reason I was there to speak to her son – explain I'd done drugs as a young man and had been able to stop those too. In this case, it appears that his young adult onset psychosis was brought on by juvenile marijuana use.

Meanwhile, I have to wait and see if my injury is permanent and whether one of the last ideas we have, one created by my son Brendan and the last young man I have at my company, Anthony, gets approved by a Canadian network, and if we're allowed to proceed with production. Given I've never asked for or collected any kind of disability, my preference would be to get back into production.

To do that we've really gone the extra mile in creating a wonderful "sizzle reel" (an example of what the show will look like) that is down in the United States at two major networks and here in Canada at another network.

I believe from the bottom of my heart that it will work out and given the time it will take to write this book, I can assure you that you will know whether I manage to close these two projects or any of the others we've presented. Now, in my case, I've had to bring other people in, to help me close deals.

> July 22, 2013
> Real Girls of New York was turned down today. We are now down to one last idea. As a result of this news, I have to practice what I preach.

If the deals don't come through, then hopefully my Ontario house will sell, and I can use those funds to move to West Vancouver and see if I might get a faculty position at a college or university there. Without any productions going, I will not be in a position to enjoy many of the pleasures that I would have, had my company worked out.

I was happy when I was young and without a lot of money, and I can be happy again. The real joys in life really are free. Most important is our relationship with our families and friends as well as our passions and hobbies, as long as they don't involve racing cars, flying planes, or taking long exotic trips to really spectacular locations around the world.

There are always *tapped out Tuesdays* (lower movie theatre ticket prices) in Canada and great deals on live theatre tickets on certain days of the week. Each community we live in has municipal facilities for residents including seniors where we can meet with people who have similar interests. I'm actually looking forward to that.

I'm also going to try my hand at writing a novel or two. Let's see if I can convert my idea for CANUSA Lodge into a novel. That's one idea I have. It was a proposed television series – a bicultural comedy, which still may be produced. I'm also going to convert my Master Degree's thesis into a novel, *Heaven Bound*.

I've also thought about doing seminars to go along with this book. I would also like to have a hand in helping set up Master Mind groups.

My first ex-wife Bev has called and we are going to drive to Nashville Tennessee to see our oldest daughter her husband and our two grandkids. It will be good to get a week off and just decompress.

My Actual Road Trip To Nashville

Franklin Tennessee:

As I'm writing this, I'm sitting at my daughter and her husband's home in Franklin Tennessee. Our drive down was really pleasant, and Bev and I were able to reconcile a lot of our old issues, letting go of the past in a very healthy and forgiving way. We were so young when we were married. Bev was a teenager. We were kids having kids.

Colleen and Rob live in a gorgeous area called Franklin. It is one of the prettiest little towns I've ever seen in my life. It is the American Dream come true.

I love Southern hospitality. One of my close friends at home in Prince Edward County, Robert, is from Memphis. My other pal Dennis and his wife

> *Paula use to live in this area. It turns out that I have a lot of connections to Tennessee, and our great, great, great uncle is buried here in the Civil War Cemetery in Chattanooga.*
>
> *The connections that we all have to one another are very significant when we begin to see just how we are all interconnected we all are at some level.*

In Conclusion

Acceptance of our powerlessness will also help us with our finances. If we find ourselves not having achieved our financial goals, the question is, what do we do about it? Do we seek alternatives to money if we don't have sufficient funds to live in the lifestyle that we think we should? A unique lifestyle might include living communally or in a cooperative housing project. Can we simplify and downsize or perhaps call it "right size", as my pal Dennis says.

What we once needed to validate ourselves materially becomes less important with time. But, I believe today that peace of mind is far more valuable than possessions. All the material goods in the world don't amount to the proverbial hill of beans if we are constantly in a state of fear and dread about our creditors and finances, fearing that we will lose what we have, or that we will not get what we want.

So, practically speaking, what can we do to get to a place of financial solvency and peace of mind? First, we must do a searching and fearless inventory of our emotional, spiritual and financial lives.

–Chapter Six–

I Believe

STEP 2. I BELIEVE
I now come to believe that a power great than myself – The Infinite Creative Intelligence - the Master Mind can change my life.

July 27th, 2013
   Well, I've just been turned down by US Cable network in New York on Real Girls of New York City. We have two options left to stay in business.
   The First is if a major network in LA says yes to us on Real Girls and we can get a Canadian broadcaster.
   Our next chance is with Canadian broadcaster and our project Contact that both Brendan and Tony created. I just opened my God file and reread the note I put in the God of my understanding box. In other words, I have a file when I run into a problem I can't seem to solve I turn it over by putting it into my God File or God box and letting go of the results.

How do I Believe - if I Don't Believe?

There are those who say, "Fake it till you make it." Okay, but how do I reconcile believing that a power greater than myself, the Master Mind, can change my life? In my own case, it has been experience. Plain and simple!

I ran on David Brady Power and self will for a long time, until I was 39 years of age. The results? Not so good.

Quite frankly, having spent so much time in California I always wished I could find a spiritual drive through center where I could go up to the window and say, "I'd like an order of peace of mind and a side order of serenity! And while you are at it, can you supersize those for me please?" That's how my brain works.

Yes, I did accomplish a great deal in my business and creative life. However, I also found myself suffering from tremendous anxiety, doubt and at times, resentment.

As a teenager and a very young man, I had an allergy to alcohol. Every time I drank I broke out in a drunk. The Irish in me I guess. I didn't realize alcoholism was a disease, analogous to type-two diabetes. I inherited it. I realized at 21 years of age that I couldn't drink and for some reason I was able to stop. I did ask the God of my misunderstanding at the time to help me stop that behaviour. But, I was not willing to surrender any other part of my life to anything outside of myself because I just didn't have enough faith in a Power greater than me.

Here was the crux of my problem: I had always sought God or wisdom - out there. In other words, it never dawned on me that I could have a Power greater than myself internally. It just seemed so odd and so foreign to my upbringing as a Catholic.

I always thought in terms of "heaven" being in the stratosphere. When you are a child in the Catholic Church you are taught they always keep the Holy Sacrament upon the altar in a tabernacle. It has a red light burning beside it and we are raised to think of it in terms of the real "Body and Blood of Jesus".

However, as a 6-year-old, I used to sit in church and stare at the tabernacle and think that there was a tunnel inside that led up to heaven, which in my child like mind, was in the stratosphere.

Then I wondered, what about the Australians? Their "out there" is my "down there". Needless to say the idea of a power greater than myself has been a lifelong journey of discovery for me.

I now feel as though I'm finally getting really close to having an absolute faith that the Master Mind (or God, in my case) can change me. However, today I believe that the spark of Divinity, the very essence of what created the universe, is within each of us and I have Michael Dowd, the author of *Thank God For Evolution,* to thank for that. His point: We are all made up of stardust. Every human being has, within his or her biology, the literal stardust that was created at the Big Bang.

All of a sudden, between his ideas and some others I was pursuing, it started to dawn on me. This is what the Preachers, Rabbi's, Imam's and Ministers had always talked about when they said, "We were made in the image and likeness of God."

It's not literal. Does God have to go to the bathroom and defecate? Pardon my crudeness, but I doubt it. But, the spark of the Divine, that infinitesimal part of us that is made up from the "spark" of God, is within each of us.

In another interesting book *Ancient Secrets of Success* by Tulshi Sen, he points out that every drop of the ocean is the ocean. If we melt ice, how do we separate what was ice from what was the water? It all flows into one.

It is my belief today that we are the Divine sparks of God manifested on this earth. And, it appears there are those who are so highly evolved, they are able to perform the miracles of the Bible. Suddenly, so much of what I'd been taught has made sense to me.

The good news today is I barely resemble the David Brady of my youth emotionally, spiritually or physically. I have grown a great deal. And, without exception, every period of growth has been preceded by a period of intense discomfort, emotional pain and often real financial challenges. I've never learned anything on a good day.

Facing the death and loss of my mother. Having my second marriage end. Losing the company I had started because I couldn't stay in it with a partner who was an active drug addict. Realizing that once again I'd set myself up to be hurt by going into business with people who couldn't be counted on to keep their word.

At the time however, it was so incredibly painful that I felt like my life would end. And here is the truth! I am not alone. How many of you who are now reading this can relate in some way to some or one of the issues I'm raising. I'm not all that different.

Who hasn't been hurt through the loss of a loved one/ family member, been through the breakup of a marriage, or experienced difficulties in business? I don't think you would be normal if you said no.

What I have to believe is that if I let go and let the Master Mind change me, then I will create the best possible outcome.

It's like the fellow who, after falling off the cliff and grabbing a branch of a tree sticking out of the rock face, with a thousand foot fall below him, looks up and prays. "Dear God, please help me." The voice says, "Let Go and Trust." The fellow then looks up and says, "Is there anyone else up there?"

Faith: it is not always easy to come by. And it's especially not easy to come by if you are a humanist, agnostic or atheist. It is even difficult if you are someone like me who has devoted a significant part of my life to being a seeker of the truth, inspiration and a conscious contact with some form of Higher Power.

One of the challenges I have is in reconciling that it is okay to ask the Master Mind specifically for help. I'm one of those people who have been influenced by the concept that it's only okay to pray for knowledge of God's will and the power to carry that out. You dare not ask for anything for yourself.

That belief is in contrast and contradiction to so many of the New Testament writings and I use them as a demonstration to me that it is okay to ask.

As an example, in Matthew 7.7 when he says, *Ask, and it shall be given you; seek, and you shall find; knock, and it shall be opened to you: For every one that asks receives; and he that seeks finds; and to him that knocks it shall be opened. Or what man is there of you, whom if his son ask for bread, will he give him a stone?*

So, here I am, a litmus test for you the reader, for by the time I finish this book, you will know whether I have been led to a place whereby I come to believe that a power great than myself, the Master Mind, can change my life. Or I will be in the proverbial toilet.

There is nothing I want more than to have my life changed. I no longer wish to feel the anxiety and fear of loss and financial insecurity that I am currently experiencing.

I also no longer desire to have to deal with individuals whose creative horizons are limited to rednecks, rock stars on crack or young women whose only claim to fame is to be the object of sensuality.

In my view there is nothing wrong with sensuality in the correct context. But, when it is one's primary purpose in life, that's not good. Those people will age, (although when I was young I never thought it would happen to me!)

The other challenge I face is that with all the work I've done, I'm stunned that I find myself here at this stage of my life. For years I've been working to change, and in fact, I have changed a great deal.

But, once again, my faulty filter is kicking in like a tantruming toddler. Perfectionism. I think that it has to be all or nothing-black or white thinking. It's counter productive, too, when I think like this.

I have changed. Are the changes going as quickly as I would like? No! One of my challenges in life is that I want everything now (patience not being a strong suit in those of us with my type of brain). When I was a young man of 20 or 21, I wanted what my then very affluent father-in-law had - a beautiful home with a pool, a Cadillac, and the ability to travel the world.

What I learned as an adult, and as I got to have many of the same things, is the amount of hard work that has to go into supporting this lifestyle. When people see my lifestyle from the outside, what they see is a man with a nice car, a home in the country, and a very comfortable apartment in midtown Toronto, who travels frequently between Toronto, California, and Europe.

Because I have a lot of flaws in my personality around faith, I don't have perfect faith. I've always been reluctant to trust that the concept of a Higher Power could change my life, because I had quite a horrible experience with my own father around being able to trust him.

As a result I made the decision at a very young age that I only would count on myself to figure everything out. The only exception was my drinking and drug use when I was younger. As I said earlier, thankfully I was willing and able to ask for help with those two issues, but not the other parts of my life.

So, the challenge is really to begin to trust that I am being taken care of. The good news is that I've come back from owing over $5 million dollars, and today I do have assets.

If I shut my company down, it will be done in an organized fashion. I will make sure that everyone knows what I am doing and what my plan is. I do have resources to get by on, but I will have to right-size my life.

How did I come to this level of understanding? By asking for help and today I do believe that I am being guided to the best solution.

I also have to be open to change, which I wasn't, for the longest time. Letting go of old ideas is arguably the most difficult thing I've ever undertaken. My mind (the faulty filter) is the evil twin brother to the dwarf Gimili from Lord of the Rings. He is the red haired one that was always going into battle and is a mighty warrior.

His evil twin brother, the Toxic Dwarf, resides in my mind and says, "Loser. You are toast. Your life will never work out. Hurl yourself off the nearest high building."

Once again, when he starts up at 5:00 a.m. when I first wake up, I now just say, "Good morning. Thank you for sharing. You can have the day off".

Fortunately I live in a bungalow in the country and only on the 5th floor of my building in Toronto. All I would do is render myself disabled. My mind is analogous to my computer booting up. Its default setting from growing up in an alcoholic home is things are not predictable or stable. Always be vigilant and aware of potential danger. Always worry because you don't know what is coming next. Be hyper-aware of your environment. Be terrified of making a mistake. Those are all perfectionist traits, which are not healthy. A psychiatrist once said to my friend, "Perfectionism is the highest form of self abuse."

You can do a lifetime of psychotherapy, one-on-one counseling, or intensive group therapy. All can support you in seeking a solution.

As well, you can have a Master Mind group and ask for help connecting with a Higher Power, or simply ask for guidance and the gift of belief. If we do believe it, we can achieve it.

We can overcome countless character defects, or flaws if you will. We can change our lives from ones of quiet desperation to lives that are much more pleasant and, dare I say, joy-filled. Does this mean you will be tiptoeing through the tulips on a daily basis? Probably not on a daily basis, but, undoubtedly your life will be much more manageable.

If I believe that the Master Mind will change my life and I humbly ask for guidance and direction to do its will, chances are that in some odd way I will find my life unexplainably correcting in such a way that problems that used to plague me will begin to straighten out.

Unexpected solutions will appear and we will see opportunities where we once saw problems. We can also stop having to think that every time we do have a problem, that we've done something wrong. We haven't. It is just a fact that life is difficult much of the time and when we try to deal with it alone, it is lonely and isolating.

Asking for help and expecting positive results will bring about change, change that will increase exponentially when we utilize the concept of the Master Mind or Divine Mind to assist us.

Furthermore, the great news is that you can create a conscious contact with the Master Mind of your choice. It's your own private concept, so you can let go of old stereotypes and ask yourself, "If I could have a personal relationship with the Master Mind or Higher Power of my choice, what would that look like?"

In my case, I started thinking about the possibility of having a friend with whom I could talk, versus buddy with the beard, the large clipboard, sitting on his throne keeping track of the 7.1 billion people on earth and making sure He/She/It knows who has been naughty or nice.

I also let go of my old idea that I was not worthy of having a connection with a Higher Power because I was so flawed, and that any self respecting Higher Power would blow me off because I am so damaged. I no longer think that.

But how many of us believe and feel that? They even have a section in the Catholic mass at Communion. *"Lord, I'm not worthy."*

With all due respect to Catholicism, I believe you are worthy. I believe this because the spark of Divinity created you and that you are "God's or the Master Mind or Divine Mind's" daughter or son. How would you treat your children? With love and respect I would hope.

–Chapter Seven–

I Am Ready To Be Changed

STEP 3. I AM READY TO BE CHANGED
I realize that erroneous self-defeating thinking is the cause of my problems, unhappiness, fears and failures. I am ready to be changed so my life can be transformed.

> *I'm sitting in Toronto now, at my apartment on Avenue Road. It is July 29th, 2013. We're in the middle of a very severe heat wave. I have the air conditioner going full tilt. It's about a quarter to four in the afternoon. I've just had some toast, a coffee and a quick lie down to get my energy up.*
>
> *I love summer. I've always loved summer probably because I was born on May 29th. I feel that we all love the season we were born in. It is just an observation on my part, with absolutely no empirical data to back that up.*
>
> *What has that got to do with the fact I am ready to be changed? Because I have a great deal of beliefs that have no basis in fact, but, rather are the culmination of data from my childhood, that I've heard when I was between three and ten years of age, and is stuck in the memory bank and it has been accepted it as gospel.*

One of my beliefs is that I am not intelligent enough, talented enough, good enough, handsome enough or lucky enough to have certain things go my way.

I don't think all of these thoughts at once. They emerge within the context of my personal and interpersonal relationships and situations in life. In spite of the fact that I have a wall full of awards and that I have produced over 130 episodes of prime time television and 4 feature films, my mind tells me it was just a fluke. Luck. Faulty filter again.

My Childhood Discovery About Charm

Where does this thinking come from? Childhood. In my case, I misinterpret what was said to me as a child. So little was understood when I was just a kid growing up in the mid 1950s. I started grade 1 in 1953. I was 6 years of age. In my first book, *Get Me To the Temple of Serenity... And Step on It!,* I told the story of the Grey Nun in Timmins (my hometown) who took me into the cloak room because I lied to her on the second day of school. I didn't want to go to school. I was terrified.

It was in that cloakroom where I saw a black and green flag that had a big elephant on it, and I said, "What's that Sister?" as she was getting ready to give me the strap for lying. She looked at it and said, "Dumbo the Safety Elephant. He's there to help you stay out of trouble."

With my big blue eyes, I looked up and said extemporaneously, "Oh Dumbo, where are you now?" She burst out laughing and did something that astounded me. She slapped her own hand and then said, "Don't ever lie to me again." I don't think I ever did after that. It was at that moment I realized that I could make people laugh, and I would go on to use that as a defense mechanism a great deal of my life.

I didn't have a great role model in my father. As I was growing up, his alcoholism was escalating. Now, I don't blame my father for how my life turned out. I am responsible for that. But, he did influence me significantly, and his behaviour did have an impact on all of us growing up in that violent, alcoholic home.

They call it dysfunctional today. What did I hear? There was fighting and emotional altercations between my mother and father. There was the threat of physical violence from my Dad to several of my siblings. There was always tension in the air. Somehow, I got it into my head that it was my fault.

> *It is now the last week of July 2013 and I am overwhelmed with fear on Monday morning. I've never worked so hard to close a deal. We have so many projects out. Will we hear this week on Contact, Myth Hunters, CANUSA Lodge, and Rock Club? The stress is unbelievable. I keep praying and asking for guidance. I need to let go. It's really difficult*

One of the many challenges I'm having about being willing to change is not to let my unhealthy old self-defeating thinking take hold. As I said previously, and it's worth repeating, when my faulty filter kicks in my mind says, "It's too late. Hurl yourself off the nearest high building."

In my thinking, it is now darkest before the dawn. However, I've been here before on several occasions. Last night I spoke to Dennis, Father John and Ron. We had dinner at Dave's Roadhouse in Prince Edward County.

It's become apparent to me that I'm holding onto my ego. While I'm willing, or I say I'm willing to let go, am I really? Apparently not! As I indicated earlier, I am always willing to let go of my drinking problem. I'm also always willing to ask my Higher Power to take care of my children.

But hold on – "my business?" I don't think so.

> *Another three days have passed. I can feel the tension mounting in me. I keep wondering, okay, what am I doing wrong? What is it that I'm not doing, right? Tony is away, and I'm here alone. I've never prayed so hard in my entire life.*
>
> *I've made the decision to drive down to my house in the country and ride out what I'm going through there. Tony is heading for a holiday with his father. I told him that he needed to be prepared not to come back to work if we can't close new business. I have to start thinking about alternative plans. I really have to think about letting go and shutting 585 Avenue Road down and just working out of my house.*

As I paraphrase the late great Gonzo journalist – Hunter S. Thompson said, *"The film and television business are a cruel, shallow money trench run by pimps and whores and where good men die like dogs: then there is also a downside to it. "*

Start The Change

What are the steps I need to take once I Ask to Be Changed? In many cases our problems are financial. How do we find a solution that will work across the board if we have little or no experience with the business of finance?

Like a business, we all need to create a spending plan. We also need to have an accurate list of our income. And it must be accurate. If you have $1,000 a month coming in, that's what you have. If you have $5,000 coming in, that is what you must plan for. If you have $10,000 a month coming in and are spending $15,000 a month because you used to always have, you are headed for a day of reckoning and a world of hurt.

Many people have magical thinking (I might be included in this category at times) and they keep spending savings trying to maintain a lifestyle that will eventually leave them insolvent, depressed and even suicidal.

However, if you are in good health and you are ambulatory then in this day and age there are many positions open to those retirees that were not open a decade or two ago. This also applies to those who are middle-aged and perhaps find themselves downsized or laid off.

What is your hobby? Do you love carpentry or decorating? Do you have a passion for renovating? Check out the large big box stores in the numerous plazas who will need folks who know what they are doing. How about writing? You can earn $25 an hour if you look for opportunities such as writing for Direct Mail businesses. How about students needing tutoring?

Were you a manager or executive in your other life? Community colleges and universities are facing retiring boomers who've done this all their lives. But, it's new and exciting for those of us who come to this calling later in life.

If your mind says, "hold on Dave, you were a big shot producer. Do you want people to see you now working for a wage?" I say to my mind, "thank you for sharing" as once again the ego (edge good out) gets in there and starts to rear his (in my case) toxic self and begin passing judgment on what it is I'm thinking of doing. I simply say, "thank you for sharing, now kindly fuck off.'

Oops, didn't see that coming did we? Please forgive my dereliction, but there are just times when it feels really good to say that. If you were a boomer! If you are one of my younger readers, my apologies and I sincerely hope I don't contaminate your young mind.

Being ready to change can include having to rethink or actually change our career path and recreate our finances to match a new lifestyle. This may be very difficult if you must make what you perceive as a downward move. You may have been a CEO, or Vice President of a large organization when you were downsized. You may have owned your own business when you had to declare personal or corporate bankruptcy.

An alcohol or drug problem may have removed you from your position as a professional and now you must rebuild your life from the ground up.

Don't let your mind stand in the way of you possibly having the best time of your life. Imagine no stress, no massive responsibility and just the chance to be a regular guy or gal that gets to meet people and find out just how wonderful they are. And of course there will always be the occasional challenging person whom we can thank for helping us learn tolerance.

There are many opportunities today to set you up as a consultant. The same with chain stores where the focus is art if you have any talent as a fine artist, potter, designer or teacher. It gets you out, and you meet new people.

If you go through this kind of "right sizing" you will need to examine your finances. When you create what I call your spending plan (or budget if you feel better using that term) you will need to create one that will allow you to have fun and include an amount dedicated to entertainment. You will also want to have an amount to take care of your basic needs and keep something in reserve in the event that you need outside help to keep your home clean.

If you have grandchildren or adult children, save a small amount so you can visit with your children or grandkids

It is very important to have a little money – fifty to two hundred dollars a month for such things as massages, counseling or chiropractic treatment that help with your overall wellbeing and self-care. Please don't isolate yourself either. Isolating for many of us is going to be a major problem especially when we've lost our friends or a loved one. We cannot sit in our homes and just vegetate. First, it will hasten your departure from the planet through a myriad of related maladies, and second, it will probably bring on a great deal of loneliness and depression.

In cities like Toronto, Los Angeles, New York, London, Sydney, Vancouver, Nashville or Calgary and I'm assuming other large cities, there will be schools teaching massage, and they will offer such treatments at a greatly reduced rate for training their massage therapists. This will be a big first step in preventing the very thing I'm alluding to in the above paragraph. It will also introduce you to self-care, a concept many of us overachievers are totally unfamiliar with. "What a waste of time" will probably be the first thought that crosses your mind. "Faulty Filter."

Here is what you need to retire in the USA as of May 2013

Retirement Statistics	Data
Average retirement age	62
Average length of retirement	18 years
Average savings of a 50 year old	$43,797
Total cost for a couple over 65 to pay for medical treatment over a 20 year span	$215,000
Percentage of people ages 30-54 who believe they will not have enough money put away for retirement	80%
Percentage of Americans over 65 who rely completely on Social Security	35%
Percentage of Americans who don't save anything for retirement	36%
Total Number of Americans who turn 65 per day	6,000
Percentage of population that is 65 years of age or older.	13%
Out of 100 people who starts working at the age of 25, by the age 65:	
Will be considered wealthy	1%
Have adequate capital stowed away for retirement	4%
Will still be working	3%
Are dependent on Social Security, friends, relatives or charity	63%
Are dead	29%
Americans older than 50 account for:	
Percent of all financial assets	77%
Percent of total consumer demand	54%
Prescription drug purchases	77%
All over-the-counter drugs	61%
Auto Sales	47%
All luxury travel purchases	80%

Amount Needed in Savings For Retirement		
Monthly income need	Savings Needed for 20 Years	Savings Needed for 30 Years
$1,000	$166,696	$212,150
$2,000	$333,392	$424,300
$3,000	$500,087	$636,450
$4,000	$666,783	$848,601
$5,000	$833,479	$1,060,751
$6,000	$1,000,175	$1,272,901
$7,000	$1,166,871	$1,485,051
$8,000	$1,333,567	$1,697,201
$9,000	$1,500,262	$1,909,351
$10,000	$1,666,958	$2,121,501

> The above sums assume your portfolio will earn a 6 percent annualized return during the course of your retirement and endure 2 percent annual inflation erosion.

We in Canada are blessed with universal health care, which eliminates over $200,000 from our costs. If you don't fit comfortably into one of the above categories, what can you do to survive? That's the question. The answer is acceptance. Otherwise, you are left with feelings of failure, low self-esteem and hopelessness. Are you really ready to be changed and let go of old erroneous self defeating thinking? This is a very difficult task to undertake.

But, you don't need to be alone. No one does. We are all worthy human beings. We are not our bank accounts, although it is a lot easier to be spiritual when you have a positive bank balance.

It is also valuable to be active in a spiritual setting like a church or fellowship of some kind where you are with positive, likeminded people. There are so many support groups today for every imaginable situation in life. And the more you can share openly and honestly with others, the less is the emotional burden on yourself. As far as finances, the fact is there are probably more people in financial need than there are who are financially solvent.

So clearly I need to let go and let God take away this unhealthy and self defeating thinking and I make a commitment to you that I will do this today.

This is just so uncomfortable to me. I find it difficult to let go of my need to control. My need to feel that I am in control is just so deeply ingrained in me that it is like making the decision to bungee jump off that super skyscraper in Dubai – your stomach comes out of your mouth it's so terrifying. I saw it on the last Mission Impossible – 18 or 105 – whichever one it was.

In Conclusion

I am ready to be changed. I am going to let go. Scary. I have so much to do to try and figure out how I will survive. But I can do this.

People who have contracted severe or life threatening illnesses may believe this kind of thinking is rubbish. However, all one has to do is go on Internet and Google how negative thinking affects our health, or the correlation between negative thinking and disease? It will astound you to see just how much our old self-defeating thinking does affect us, and the outcome of our medical treatments. It has been proven time and time again in these empirical medical studies that our thinking has a significant bearing on the outcome of our treatment, especially if one has been prone to self-pity, anger, resentment or jealousy most of their lives. These emotions are poison to our system and we need to let go of them and the sooner the better.

–Chapter Nine–

I Decide to be Changed

STEP 4. I DECIDE TO BE CHANGED
I make a decision to surrender my will and my life to the Master Mind. I ask to be changed at depth.

Facing Financial Challenges

If you don't have the resources to live independently, then you are in the company of roughly three quarters of North Americans who don't have enough. Take heart, you are not alone. We have to come up with a new paradigm for aging and living quality lives by reallocating resources in an intelligent way. We have to, or the societal, physical and emotional costs are going to be staggering.

We're not all going to be spending the winter in Florida, California or some other sunny place. But, with a group of friends, using some old-fashioned ingenuity we may be able to come up with some alternatives. What about doing something like finding a car service where they pay you to drive a car from whatever city you are in to Florida, California, or Arizona? You could spend a week or two enjoying the warm weather there by cutting your costs and sharing a place just like you did when you were young.

Even if you can't, it doesn't mean you are worthless or a burden. We all have gifts, regardless of our financial circumstances, especially if we have a positive mental attitude, an ability to go with the flow and seek guidance in our lives when we feel powerless. That is being changed at depth.

We have to alter our view of family, aging and what it means to allow future generations to age with dignity. It has only been in the last generation that the idea of not caring for the elderly within the family has taken precedent. It was those of us - we boomers - who blew our aging parents off, metaphorically, and in some cases, literally.

I'm afraid that, for many of us, we're about to discover that as we do unto others, it is done unto us. When we are young, we feel invincible. We feel independent. We want what we want, and we want it now. To a large degree we have become a very self-centered, selfish generation who are about to pay the price for our lack of caring.

And it's going to be brutal if we don't shift our view on taking care of others and asking to be changed at depth. As it turns out there are many universal laws that we thought we could flaunt in our younger years, and now they've come home to roost. Oops! Didn't see that coming.

So, what is the answer? What is our hope? Well, one of the tools we can use to help us get back on course is the Eight Steps.

We all need company and support. We all need love and compassion. Let's begin practicing with each other – even when we're occasionally upset with those closest to us.

> *Okay, shifts happen. It's August 15th.*
>
> *I'm sitting on Air Canada in Executive First. This is a complete gift to me as I'm on a real discount airfare. However, I was up at 4 a.m. to catch this flight to Vancouver. I simply asked for an aisle seat, and they bumped me to First Class. Yeah Air Canada!*
>
> *I'm on this flight because while meditating I had a thought, "why not see if one of the universities in Vancouver would consider having you teach in their film program"? And there was a notice for a part time teaching position. Ten hours per week.*
>
> *I've done it before very successfully. I've had a written goal that I want to move back to West Vancouver for years now. I did put an add on one of the Internet sites. As a result I was able to rent my furnished house for 3 months, the length of the teaching contract. I'm one of three people being interviewed tomorrow. I have no idea if I will get it or not?*

I've been totally open with my banks and creditors. Here's the miracle. Once I accepted that shutting down was inevitable, a calm has come over me. I don't know if I will get the position, but stay tuned and I will let you know.

Self-Defeating Thinking

Here is what I know today. Three weeks ago my old self-defeating thinking took over, and I couldn't see a way out of where I was. I felt hopeless and defeated.

I mentioned this to my close friends that night at Dave's Road House, and they managed to talk me through the process. That kind of thinking is disastrous not only to me, but to my children and my family as well. They just worry themselves over my mental attitude. Yet, in my willingness to be changed, I have to be rigorously honest with myself. That is how I felt.

I'm shocked, sitting and reflecting on this airplane that I felt that way. But, I did. And, now it's gone. I'm actually feeling quite good. More and more, things are turning around right now.

However, my old self-defeating thinking reappears: "David, you are not good enough; you are not smart enough; talented enough; funny enough; young enough to be hired by a university. What about your age? Who are you trying to kid?"

These were the thoughts I initially had when I sent the email out to the university. Actually, I sent two in a row because I tried to write one while I was in a meeting and ex-wife number two always said to me (and I said this in the second email), "David, you are a man. Men can't do two things at the same time. Please learn to accept that." Damn, she's right.

Here are the facts: I have a wealth of real world experience. I am a rock solid teacher with tremendous experience both in and out of the classroom. I've been blessed with a real gift of communication. I also enjoy being around young people as they are so full of energy and enthusiasm and remind me of myself when I was there age.

I am according to my own children, a wonderful man who cares a lot about people. They have also told me their friends love coming to our office and hanging out with us. They think I'm cool. That's so funny to me, but in a warm way.

We are constantly having students around our productions because I believe in mentoring them. I can remember how difficult it was for us when we started out and I can still remember the few "Hollywood-type" producers and directors who would take the time to speak to us as though we were human beings and not a pain-in-the-ass.

I've been sitting here on the plane preparing my lecture, which is part of the interview process, "What is story?"

I could easily be depressed if I don't get the job tomorrow, but, at this moment, I'm feeling fairly positive because regardless of what happens, I believe that I am willing to let go of all that unhealthy thinking that has caused me so many problems in the past. I am willing to let go and trust that my new Master Mind centered thinking will allow me to find solutions to my problems that I've not had before.

Learning to Trust the Master Mind

Three weeks ago I couldn't believe there was a solution out of the mess I was in. I did an inventory, and realized, okay, I have a house. I have equity. I have savings and investments: I'm not going to starve today, even though my mind (faulty filter) believes it will. I am ready to believe that my life can be transformed, and I am now ready to let go and let my Higher Power change me.

I believe that I am being guided to my greatest good. Even though I can't see it at this very moment, there is no problem that can't be solved by trusting in my Higher Power,

One of my other concerns is that I also have a residence in Toronto. Do I give it up? Do I keep it when I sell my house? As of today we still have one last hope for production.

> 10:00 a.m. August 15th
> We were just turned down by USA Network on my CANUSA Lodge. I will write it as a novel I think. So, that leaves us with a potential six hours on a series called Contact.
> If it comes through I've decided that I will turn the production over to Mike, who has been with me for almost seven years. I will also have my son Brendan and Tony who developed it be the primary source of creativity.

As I may have said before, I have a friend who I've worked with for many years, and she can direct at least three of them. I might direct the other three.

> *It's 5:45 on August 15th. I'm sitting looking at Horseshoe Bay British Columbia. I have just taken a picture of one of the most beautiful sights one can ever see. The cloud covered peaks of the Costal Range and the harbor in the background. It's starting to rain, so I guess I will get back to the car and continue my writing in a café.*
>
> *I've just had dinner at Troll's Fish N Chips. It is a landmark in Horseshoe Bay and has been since 1946. I've decided to sit in the rain and enjoy nature. Tonight I will hang out to stay awake so I will sleep in until at least 6 or 7 tomorrow morning.*
>
> *So, becoming ready to be changed. Today I saw a beautiful apartment in West Vancouver on Bellevue. This is the street that runs along the shoreline of the Pacific Ocean and looks over English Bay from West Vancouver. It is a little on the expensive side. The good news is, the manager said he's flexible. I will see what they say tomorrow at the university.*

I've been reading my notes, and I sincerely hope that the research, the reading and the writing that I've done will lead me to a place of being able to demonstrate to the faculty members that I know what I am doing, and that I am anxious to do the best job possible. At least I've taken the time to prepare.

However, unlike in the old days, I'm perfectly okay letting go and trusting that I will be guided to change so that my life can be transformed. I am so hopeful that my life will change. Sitting here in one of the most beautiful locations on earth makes me realize how much I want to live here. A huge seagull has landed about six feet from me and is just sitting on the railing looking at me. It's as if it's welcoming me back home.

A sizeable BC Ferry is just pulling out and heading over to Nanaimo, the city where my sister Trish her husband Chris live. I will be back here Tuesday to have lunch with them.

The rain has passed. The clouds are lying in layers, like giant blankets in mid air – and rising above the verdant mountainside. Beautiful. It is just so beautiful. In the past, I would seldom sit and just enjoy the beauty of nature. I was always in too big a hurry, too busy as I always had to be somewhere. I am committed to letting go and trusting that I will be guided to the next right steps.

I received an email today from my financial partner. He wants to talk to me in person. I understand that too. He has been such a gentleman.

I have a lot on my plate. I truly recognize that I must stay in the day. When I think about tomorrow, I lose the peace of this moment. When I think about yesterday and all the things I didn't accomplish, I become distracted from the beauty surrounding me. Right now, right here I have enough. I am good enough. I am so grateful to be here.

One of my greatest challenges is to accept myself as I am. I am not perfect.

> *Friday, August 16th.*
> *I have an interview at the university. It is at 3:15 today. I've just gone over my lecture again. It's 6:15 in the morning. I did get to sleep in by staying awake last night even though my body thinks it's 9:15 with the time change.*
>
> *Again, I'm sitting this morning thinking this is odd, as I've never really gone for an interview before. When I taught in the past, they were just happy to have me come down and teach. This is getting a real job. I feel pretty good about the material. If I'm successful, it's because I took the time to prepare. If I don't, it's because I'm not the right person for the job. Not because I've done something wrong. That is a healthy change for me. How do I move out here so quickly? If we don't get our 6-hour series, I have to give notice on my apartment in Toronto and pay one more month's rent, but do I want to make two drives across Canada? I don't think so although I'm going to have to drive my car out if I don't haul it out on the back of a moving truck.*
>
> *So, I am trying to approach this differently than I would have in the past. Perhaps I can seek some feedback from folks who've had to make these moves. I thought, just get rid of apartment furniture. I will go online and see how much a truck is from Toronto to Vancouver. If I had to do that twice, it would be brutal.*
>
> *I will wait until the house sells and just pick up some used furniture in Vancouver. I will put*

> my things into storage. I am ready to be changed and let go of my old self-defeating thinking.

Romance

This is one area where I don't feel qualified to speak, given my track record. Nonetheless, I have to look at where else am I ready to change. Romantic relationships have been a challenge for me. I may not be alone. However, in the case of Deb, we were married twenty years. We are still very close, but it took a great deal of work to get through it. With my first wife, we were kids having kids. As I mentioned earlier, Bev wasn't even out of her teens when our son was born.

What is interesting, and makes me think that there may be something to the old karmic wheel, is what has happened to me with my relationship in the States. Here is what I would do all the time in the past. A woman would have strong feelings for me – now, I'm talking about three women, over fifteen years – from ages 23 to 39, until I got remarried. I was focused on my career in the film business and travelled all the time. In each case, these women would express their affection for me, and I'd say the very thing that was just said to me. I'm not interested in getting married. I'm not interested in a domestic situation. I've been on my own for 'X' number of years, and I like it. But if you want to keep it casual and we could see each other once in a while that would be good.

The difference is that I do want to meet someone I can love and be with today. But I am grateful for the time I had with Kathy for the two and a half years we saw each other. She is a wonderful woman with a great family.

One of the humorous things near the end of my being single is that I was seeing two women, one in NYC and a woman in LA. I told both of them about each other as I always prided myself with being upfront and honest. Well, they got together. Ouch!!!! Talk about getting caught in the crossfire. However, I'm close to both of them today, or at least I've visited with both of them and they seem to have forgiven me for being such a complete jerk (which I was back then). Ironically, my friend Celeste, who is one of these women, just called me the other day and she confirmed that I was a very decent human being. Nice.

I believe we can all laugh about it today.

> *Well, it's Wednesday, August 21st. My interview went very well. I'm about to fly back to Toronto this morning. I had decided to wait in Vancouver until today to see if I were going to be fortunate enough to get the position. I thought if I do, at least I could lock down an apartment, organize my move and have some degree of certainty. Apparently, it's not to be. Yet, I feel okay about it. I was asked to get some letters of recommendation. I will take that as a positive sign.*

Wednesday August 28th, 6:00 pm.

Originally, they were going to do all the interviews on Friday, but one was postponed until today. So, I will not know today as I had hoped. In the meantime, I was able to contact the former Chair of Ryerson University where I taught, and he's written a very strong letter of support for me.

I've received a beautiful letter from my longtime friend and associate George Flak. It almost brought me to tears, as his description of me is just so generous and caring.

The executive from Bravo!, who approved our Yonge Street, Toronto Rock & Roll Stories also wrote a very nice letter for me. Ten or fifteen years before she'd been a student of mine at Ryerson.

I have put a deposit down on an apartment in West Vancouver. It's not the nicest apartment I saw, but, I can afford it and it has a beautiful view of the ocean and the Vancouver skyline. And, I can walk to all the stores and restaurants in West Vancouver. I have to stay away from the Pie Store on Marine Drive though. Dear God in heaven, they make the best damn apple pie. But, if I keep going back I will be 200 pounds and a type 2 diabetic. But, it is unbelievably good.

What was interesting is just how nervous I was about doing my interview. Having always been the one who was interviewing, it was a real turn of events.

Same Day,

I am now back at the apartment in Toronto. I'm grateful to say that I will meet my brother

> Robert tomorrow who is in from Sault Ste. Marie and we will head down to my house in Sandhurst. He has a truck with him so I might be able to move a few things out of Avenue Road to the house if we don't have word today from Vision on our potential 6 hours.

It Really Works!

> Thursday August 29th, 10 PM
>
> I am at my house in Sandhurst Ontario with my brother Robert. My good friends Dennis and Paula just live east of the Ferry, and they are two of the folks I really depend on for emotional and spiritual support.
>
> I spend a great deal of my time in Picton, which is in "the County" as it is affectionately referred to. I love this part of Eastern Ontario, and I always said to people it's because it's as close as I can get to the West Coast.
>
> I just received the call from the search committee, and I've been offered the position in Vancouver.
>
> I need to be in Vancouver on Tuesday September 3rd. Dear God in Heaven. How am I going to do this?
>
> It's what I had hoped for. It's also looking like what I'm preaching does work. That's really encouraging. I would have been very embarrassing not to have these steps work.
>
> I can't even begin to put into words what this week has been like. It's been three days since I got the call.

> *If I never believed in the power of the Master Mind before, I do now. My ex-wife Deb will help organize my move out of 585 Avenue Road. I have talked to Tony, my former assistant, and he will organize the physical move of the furniture into storage so my son Brendan can have it on his return from Vancouver.*
>
> *I've taken my car in to get new tires and to get new brakes as driving through the mountains can be dangerous.*
>
> *The two young women who are graduate students at Queens and the University of Toronto in Electrical Engineering are moving into my house today as I'm on my way up to Toronto this afternoon with my car packed full of clothes, and I have more there to pick up. Wow. I am feeling so much stress just trying to figure out how to get all this done in a matter of two days.*

My friend Pete, who works at Ontario Power Generating, has posted on the company bulletin board that my house is up for sale. I got word that they are going to build the new power plant just east of my home. There will be new folks moving into the area and someone will like it. I've done so much renovation work to the house.

Stress While Asking For Change

Let's talk about stress. How much stress do I think I have? Mega stress, metastress; stress of stress? What about all the possible challenges trying to move to Vancouver with five days notice? I will have to move from not one, but two homes in two different cities – my house in the country and my place in Toronto. Combine that with not knowing about my company's future and, boy, do I feel stress.

I have committed to make the decision to be changed, and I am surrendering my will and my life to the Master Mind. I ask to be changed at depth.

Okay, it's been about fifteen seconds. There has been no angelic choir singing in my head. There was a flash of light a few days ago on the flight back from Vancouver, but it was when the captain turned the plane to starboard, and we got a glimpse of the rising sun. However, I did get a sense of excitement.

Practically speaking, what does this all mean? First and foremost, I made the decision over 13 months ago really to try a version of this Step. I made a commitment to a group of friends that I was going to try surrendering and seeking my Higher Power's will in my life. Do I know who this Divine Power is? No! But, if there is one, I'm sure He/She knows me. Since then I have asked every day to be changed. I've learned to be careful what you pray for as you might get it, and change can be both frightening and uncomfortable.

I have made this point before, but it is imperative I let go of old ideas. This is not as easy as it sounds. Whenever you make a declaration to change certain behaviours in your life, have you ever noticed that the very things you want to change seem to appear right in your face?

I ask for patience, and I'm surrounded by slow pokes in traffic. I realize that I'm the one sitting there fuming while a nice couple are just out for a drive, and I'm pounding on my steering wheel because I have to get the car home so I can sit down and read my emails. Hello! This is not critical.

Or, I worry endlessly and needlessly. I obsess whether someone likes a project that I've created.

I am powerless over the fact that I was physically disabled by the assault on me. I have flare-ups of anger at times because I feel life is unfair. The fact is life is unfair a lot of the time. I need to surrender this behaviour and all my self-defeating thinking to the Master Mind. It is my only hope for real peace of mind and happiness.

More importantly, I really need to let go of old thinking around money, property and prestige. It is something I'm still very attached to.

However, as I alluded to earlier, I need to get right-sized about it. I'm no longer going to have a couple of residences for the time being. My very nicely renovated home with the comfortable deck on which I could sit and watch the water, and the birds, is going. But, it's my choice.

> *I've had to really let go of results in that area with over 300 executives saying "no" to me. I am powerless over their decisions, and my ego wants to me to strike out at them for*

> *doing their jobs. It does feel unfair. If I had failed on a bunch of projects, that would be one thing. But I haven't.*
>
> *How willing am I to be changed? I seem to have run out of options in that area, and I'm down to the last possibility for now with potential productions. Could it change? Absolutely. Will it change? I have no idea at this moment.*

I just spoke to a network executive who once worked for me. He is now at one of the major channels. I asked him, "What about the proposal I handed you?" I told him, "I need you to be honest." He said, "Okay, it's just like everyone else's. I've got three ideas that are exactly the same. There is nothing in the idea you submitted that will make it stand out, like yours used to." There it is. Proof that my brain is damaged. I always was able to knock these proposals out of the park. Time and time again. Where does this leave me?

So, how do I make the decision to be changed? By letting go of the need to control. It is very interesting letting go of control and outcomes. Every part of me wants to rebel at this concept as my whole life, I've always felt that if I don't take control, take charge, no one will be able to do what needs to get done. In my own case, I began changing when I hired a very competent young man about 7 years ago. While he's not perfect, he is incredibly capable and intelligent. I can trust him to make good decisions.

I don't know about any of you who are reading this book, but I need to recognize that the endless chatter that is going on in my mind is just a complete waste of time and energy: *"moving, money, Vancouver, Toronto, Sandhurst, my relationship that's gone south on me, my health, aging, car repairs, selling the house, not selling the house, death, the dentist, writing this book, wanting to be of service, will I ever get laid again? Maybe some apple pie with ice cream, hoping I do well in the teaching position, telling them I really want this."*

The endless chatter just keeps rolling along basically in one variation or another of the aforementioned. I just have to stay in the habit of thanking my mind for sharing when it starts on this rampage.

If I am to be successful doing this Step, I must step out in faith. I must be willing to turn the results over to the Master Mind while also be willing to do the work myself. In other words, I can't just sit around thinking, "Okay, here is my order God, can I have it by Friday?"

As an example, what just happened to me? A few weeks ago I made the sincere declaration I want to change my life and myself. What did I do to accomplish that?

First, I had to have a goal and declare it. Then I had to take action and move toward it. As I was meditating, I had the overwhelming sense to go online and check for a teaching position. When I saw that there was an opening at a university, I couldn't believe it. I had to write a letter expressing my desire to teach. When the woman called me the following week to say they wanted to interview me, I had to buy the plane ticket to fly out to Vancouver. Then I had to make a call to my second oldest friend, who just happens to live in Vancouver, to see if anyone had a place at which I could stay. He suggested I call another old friend. When I did telephone Tim, he said he would be away that week and was happy to have me stay in his condo/studio in Vancouver. Tim also left me his Smart car. It all just fell into place.

I did the planning and turned the results over to the Master Mind. It seems to have gone effortlessly. I found a potential residence where I could leave a deposit until Friday of that week. In the event that I don't get the teaching position I will be able to get my deposit back. If I do get it, I have secured a place to live.

What I learned from that experience is that, if I'm willing to ask to be changed at depth and to turn my will and life over to the Master Mind, I will be guided to the best possible outcome. This is what I ask for every day now.

It's obviously easy to be changed at depth when everything is going your way. It's not when all you hear is no, and all you seem to experience is disappointment. It is baffling to me. Yet what I do know is that people have this faith, and those who desire to be changed at depth are happier human beings, even when things are not going their way! They have faith that it will turn around.

This is one of the things that I find interesting about researchers in the social or behavioural sciences. They usually don't take into account that people of faith have a measurable quality of life that is vastly different from people who do not.

I want to be changed. I don't want to be plagued by fear and doubt anymore. I don't want to lie awake at night wondering, "Will I end up penniless, homeless, alone? Will I ever find anyone to love who will love me back unconditionally? Will I ever find true peace of mind? Will I be able to repay my investors and creditors from my production company?"

These are questions that I am now asking to have guidance about by being changed at depth, so I no longer do what I've done in the past that has led to this situation that I am in.

I have changed a great deal as I said in the previous chapter. I've not had a drink of alcohol in over 44 years, and I've not touched a mood altering substance in nearly 30 years. I've stopped being a 'rage-a-holic', decades ago. I've stopped being irresponsible many decades ago. I have saved money. I have repaid an enormous amount of debt and have cleared up the wreckage of my past, by and large.

I know I can change. That said, this is like the PhD of letting go and surrendering. While I was always willing to ask the Master Mind to help me, I still kept running the show. It was not a conscious decision: I just didn't realize that this is what I was doing. Now I know and actually hope to be able to let go completely, and really just trust that every part of my life will work out, regardless of what the short term looks like. And I sincerely hope this includes dying when the time comes. I know that it will come eventually and that I must make friends with death. Not in a macabre way but, in the realization that death is a natural part of living that we all must pass through.

What I find interesting is that since I did make that decision 13 or 14 months ago, my life has taken a free fall into uncertainty.

Consider the old adage, "Be careful what you pray for." As with any journey in life, we must all confront our demons if we are ever to overcome them. As Joseph Campbell talks about in the hero's journey, we first have to come face-to-face with our single greatest enemy, our minds (ego), and overcome both the internal and external challenges of life.

> *To review: It is now September 10, 2013. Wow! Time is flying by. I'm sitting in my very comfortable apartment in West Vancouver. My first day of the university last Wednesday, September 3rd, there was a torrential downpour. I got soaked when I didn't know where to park and where I left my car was about 10 minutes from the building where I was to be. But, I dried out in time for commencement gathering. Lesson one: It rains a lot in Vancouver. Bring an umbrella and raincoat.*
>
> *Since then it has been sunny and warm. Outside my window in West Vancouver I can look at English Bay and see right across to UBC. There are numerous ships moored in the harbor. This is one of the most beautiful cities on earth, if not the most beautiful. I can see the mountains of Vancouver Island in the distance.*
>
> *My first two classes, last Wednesday and Thursday, went very well. I really enjoyed*

> *being with all the young men and women who were excited to be at a University and ready to learn. So many of them were like me. They'd been out in the world and now had come back. As I'm writing this, one of the endless seaplanes has just taken off and flown right past my apartment that has floor to ceiling glass windows. I feel so blessed.*
>
> *I have had to organize and move so much in such a short time. How did it work out? So far, so good! I've tried not to be the way I was in the past and worry so much. I keep simply letting go of expectations and observing my mind.*
>
> *I am such a chronic worrier. How will I get everything into the apartment by myself? I asked to be changed at depth and then I ask for help. The two young men who take care of this building are only too happy to help me unload my car.*

People were amazed that I was doing this trip alone with my car so fully packed, the only room in it was for me to sit in the drivers seat. Every spare inch (or centimeter ... I am Canadian) was filled with personal things I would most need. The upside was I got to see some of the most beautiful sights I've ever seen. I love the Midwest, and the folks were just so incredibly friendly. I love America. I really do.

By letting go, I did move two places. I did let go of my apartment in Toronto. I did manage to pack what I needed to survive in Vancouver until I could either move my furniture out from Sandhurst, or sell my house furnished (which has not happened yet). Thank God for IKEA. I've got all I need to make it through now.

I've also been able to see a lot of very old friends whom I knew as a young man in the 1970s and 1980s, when I first moved to Vancouver. At this very moment, the question I have is practically speaking, how do I ask to be changed at depth?

First, I need a Master Mind group, those likeminded folks whom I can count on to support me through this process. I want to get a new perspective on my life. I really have so much to be grateful for. And whenever things don't go my way, it's not personal. The universe doesn't have it in for me. So many wonderful things have happened in my life. I've loved the fact I've been able to travel the world and meet some of the most interesting people alive including world renowned scientists, members of the British Royal Family, a few Prime Ministers, Hollywood stars and legends of Rock & Roll. However, it has not given me the peace of mind or happiness that I want. It's been exciting. It's been interesting. It certainly has given me a lot of great stories to share with my students.

What Have I Really Learned?

Furthermore, it has been a tremendous learning opportunity. If there is one thing I am so grateful for, it is for all the wisdom I have acquired through my travels and my work. I have been engaged in a lifetime of learning, as a result of all the research I've had to do on many of the documentary series I have written and produced or directed. One of the remarkable things I've enjoyed is learning about the world around me. I've been able to acquire knowledge that is not readily available in our current culture. Some of the teachings I've acquired have caused me a lot of discomfort because they shook my religious beliefs to the core. I do believe they will pay off in the long run if I have the courage to examine some of these tenets from a mature point of view.

These studies have also forced me to change my old thinking and embrace new concepts. I've had to keep an open mind and listen to what others who don't agree with me have to say. This is really being changed at depth.

Is it is earth shattering? No, but it is relevant to this discussion. If I am always fixated on being right, or a know it all, or being such a control freak that I drive people away from me, then chances are I will live a very lonely and isolated life. The question I would ask myself is, would you rather be right or happy?

Asking to have myself changed can lead to temporary discomfort. Letting go of old ideas can be a painful experience, especially if one's identity is tied up in those ideas.

I am not my job. I am not my physical self because my physical self is always in a state of transformation. I have a new stomach lining in five days, my skin is replaced every six weeks, and all of my molecules are in a constant state of transition. I am an entirely new me biologically every seven years.

That is part of who I am. I am not my limbs, I am not my brain, although that is a very important part of who I am. I'm not just Andrew, Colleen, Brendan and Laurel's father, as well as Sophie, Guerin, Henry and Conlan's granddad. I'm not just Liz, Trish, Robert and Jim's brother. But, I am a member of that family as well as being connected, whether I know it or not, to our greater family - the rest of humanity. We are all the sum total of all humanity that has lived before us.

I'm the sum total of the original big bang that went off billions of years ago. We've all emerged from the primordial ooze that came into existence during the earth's formative years.

I know there are those who really believe the earth is only ten thousand years old. I respectfully disagree, and the preponderance of hard science backs up my belief. I worry that some of these beliefs and faith are built on quick sand. They may eventually give way at some point in the future. I believe they have to. Again, as Michael Dowd so adequately explains in his wonderful watershed treatise, *Thank God for Evolution*, he went from being an Evangelical Preacher who really believed the fact that the earth was created in seven days, ten thousand years ago, and then came to and realized, how is that possible?

I think what is really important is to recognize the truth in all world's religions. Each faith, whether Christian, Jewish, Hindu or Muslim, is based on ancient myth and metaphor. However, just because they are based on myth and metaphor doesn't mean that there isn't real substance and truth to them.

In closing this chapter, I want to say that if someone could prove to me that this thinking is flawed, I'd be willing to examine it and change those beliefs.

–Chapter Nine–

I Forgive

STEP 5. I FORGIVE
I forgive myself for all my mistakes and shortcomings. I also forgive all other persons who may have harmed me.

If ever there were a difficult principle to practice, forgiveness has to be it. When I have resentment or am angry with someone for what I perceive they've done to me, I tie up all of my life's energy. If I'm unwilling to forgive them and accept them just the way they are, I'm in for a heap of trouble.

I love the line about resentment – I drink poison and wait for them to die. Does this mean we accept inappropriate behaviour? Absolutely not!

We have a responsibility to ourselves, and others especially our children or grandchildren, to protect them from any form of abusive behaviour whether it is physical, emotional, sexual, or psychological.

We live in a society that suggests revenges is a dish best served cold. We are inundated by mass media messages about people who devote a great deal of energy to insure that they are able to get back, or get even at their former friends, spouses, or enemies for perceived wrongs that have been done to them.

The Challenges
(And there are many)

Here's the problem. NONE OF US IS PERFECT! All right, you may be the one exception. Generally speaking, we are all perfectly imperfect. Do most people harm us intentionally? I really don't think so. There are those who definitely lack empathy, and there are sociopaths and psychopaths, many of whom are running large and successful corporations. They cannot understand why people feel victimized by them when they fire them, shut companies down to maximize profits, or make themselves the center of attention.

The tragedy in Lac Megantic, Quebec, was a telling example. Here, you had a CEO, a man who had reduced the train's crew down to one person, who had to do the jobs that several men had done in the past. One of their trains rolls into a town, creates a burning inferno killing fourty seven men, women and children and destroying the lives and homes of countless others, and the CEO goes on national television in the US and Canada and complains how no one appreciates that he's come to Canada to see the damage for himself.

He cannot fathom the harm he's created or the tragic and negative consequences that his actions had by reducing the number of employees on a train. His goal was to maximize profits. The question that will be examined in the years to come will be, was this an avoidable tragedy? And, he gets upset on national television because the people of the town are angry with him and says, "I'm never coming back here again."

However, no one in town will ever find peace until they can forgive him. That doesn't mean he should get away with not accepting some responsibility for the events of that July night. Whether he or the engineer will face criminal or civil actions in a court of law, is to be determined.

Nelson Mandela who recognized the need for forgiveness never looked back in anger at the men who had robbed him of the majority of his adult life. He came out of prison and led South Africa through arguably one of the most remarkable political transformations known in history.

There were no reprisal murders, no violence, and no widespread civil disobedience. And, did the white South African's go through a very challenging time? I suspect none of us who were there will ever know. But, they did it.

Yet, that is what living with anger or resentment is like. We must forgive everyone in our lives if we are truly to find happiness. Again, no one is immune from this basic human emotion. We all have it. I suspect even Mother Theresa had it at times.

What happens frequently is we are unable to forgive ourselves for things we've done in the past. This is a double-edged sword, too. It robs us of life's energy and joy. It is really important to recognize that we are worthy human beings.

We all make mistakes. Some of us have done really terrible things in the past. Others of us had just done the normal things - yelled at our children, gossiped about someone we didn't like, lied to someone, stole something when we were children, but, we feel we are the only ones who could have done anything this bad.

You may have cheated on your spouse. You may have cheated on your expense account at work. One of the great things about a Master Mind Group is that we can befriend someone that we really trust and share this information with them and finally experience relief.

Possible Solutions

We may be Catholic or Anglican and turn to the sacrament of reconciliation. We can go to our minister or a friend and just acknowledge our wrongdoing. It is vital for peace of mind and healthy self-esteem to unburden ourselves of these typical flaws.

Is there anything new here I'm saying? Absolutely not! It's been known since the beginning of recorded history. In Matthew 18:21-22 when Peter asks Christ if he should forgive someone seven times, Christ responds not seven times but seventy-seven times.

In other words, forgiveness has to be infinite. We must continue to forgive those who've harmed us because otherwise we allow anger and resentment go grow inside of us like a cancerous cell. It will eventually eat you alive and rob you of your peace of mind and true happiness. And the good news is because we forgive, so we are forgiven.

How do we forgive, especially when we have really been betrayed? Perhaps our spouse has cheated on us, perhaps our friends have taken advantage of our generosity and then done something that has hurt us deeply. Perhaps we've loaned money to someone close to you, and they've not paid you back or taken responsibility for the loan.

Perhaps we've been lied about and hurt in business by someone we really trusted and thought was our friend. Any one of these events is enough to cause any one of us a great deal of pain and suffering. Our instinct is to strike back in anger and get even. First we have to make sure that our faulty filter has not been at work

Here's the rub. We only end up hurting ourselves when we stay angry with someone. In my opinion, here are the facts. No one gets away with anything in life. While certain people may enjoy a temporary benefit from taking advantage of us or hurting us, eventually, it comes back on the perpetrator.

It may take some time, but, enviably, a price has to be paid by all of us for our deeds. By the way, this is true of positive behaviour too. The South Asians call it the law of Karma. We in North America have a phrase: "what goes around comes around."

The fact is those who commit this offence eventually end up paying a price for it. No one really gets away with anything in this life. Period! These are indisputable laws of nature. The universe is set up like this, in my opinion. We as a species continue to try and circumvent these laws and time-after-time, we are taught lessons.

Can we consciously connect our behaviour to past events? You can do a simple test in your own life. Think of a time, when you have gossiped or said something about someone you didn't like or who had hurt you. Now, think about a time when some days, weeks, months or years later, you found yourself on the receiving end of the same behaviour.

Think of a time when you've known someone who was doing something that you knew was immoral, or dishonest. At first it appears that they were getting away with it. Then what happens? They get caught and find themselves on the receiving end of similar actions. It is a closed loop. It is an energy source that must complete its cycle. Right actions lead to right outcomes. The outcomes may not happen immediately, but they will if we keep working toward them.

This is why it is important for us to be proactive in resolving our differences with others. Practically speaking, what can we do?

All right, let's say a good friend hurts us in business. Let's say this is a person who we have really bent over backwards to help. Then they end up not only lying about us, and they manage to really cripple us emotionally because we feel so hurt. Worse yet, they may end up running off with our sweetheart or our business. Initially, it won't be easy to forgive them, and we might say a prayer like, "Dear God, bless that black hearted bastard Harry, because I can't."

It's a start. I'm not saying we have to have perfection; I'm suggesting as it's been suggested before, "progress, not perfection."

After a number of days, weeks, or years, we may be able to muster up, "Dear God, take any resentment or anger I feel toward Harry, and please grant him peace of mind and the best outcome in his life."

Conversely, if you have gossiped or cheated or stolen from someone you may have to go to them and clean up your side of the street. This is not an action to be taken lightly. And, this is exactly where a Master Mind group can support you in taking the correct action.

You may need to sit down and look at your part in it. If you've been cheating with your best friend's wife or husband, I don't know that it is a good idea to go up and say to either spouse, "I've been sleeping with your wife/husband and I'm sorry."

First, you are leading with your chin and it is likely you will receive a slap in the face, or worse, destroy a marriage. Did his wife ask you to do this? Seek guidance again from your Master Mind partners, as you don't want to bring harm on a third party.

You cannot seek your own peace of mind at the expense of another. It may be appropriate to declare to your Master Mind partners, I have been doing this behaviour. I request that all of you pray for me to get the spiritual guidance and help I need to stop.

You may have harmed someone in business. You may have gossiped or lied about someone or spread false rumors about their integrity when you were angry with them.

With the guidance of your Master Mind partners, you may set up a time visit the person you've harmed. Regardless of what flaws they have you are not there to discuss their weaknesses or personality traits. You are there to clean up your part in whatever situation has arisen. Often when we do this, amazing things happen. People are overwhelmed by your honesty and forthright admission, and we see a healing take place right in front of our eyes.

And Now, Let's Talk About Death!

Just in case you were starting to really feel too good, I thought I should bring a little feedback into the discussion to keep us all stabilized.

When I was a young man in the insurance business, I noticed when I said to a young woman "It's no joke to croak if you are broke" they just headed for the hills. There's not a lot we can say humorously about this subject except what Woody Allen has said. We do need to look at the importance of cleaning up our relationships with our family or close friends before we die. How many of us will leave this planet with unresolved differences with our immediate family members? I suspect a number of us.

Whether we are talking about brothers and sisters, or sons and daughters or in-laws or extended family or ex husbands or wives it would be in all of our best interests to clean these relationships up. We've all had disagreements with our siblings, or children, parents or friends. But, is that how you want to be remembered? I don't. In my own case, I had to make amends to my oldest children from my first marriage. I'd moved out to Vancouver to attend university and stayed for 12 years. As a result, I didn't really participate in their upbringing. I was an absent Dad. It took a significant amount of time, and the willingness to keep reaching out. To my children's credit, they were very gracious in their forgiveness of me. But, it took time.

When I was young, I used to apologize for getting up in the morning. I was always sorry. It was a constant state.

As I matured, people didn't want to hear how sorry I was, they wanted to see action. When I lost a great deal of money in 1986, I couldn't stand saying I was sorry any longer for the movie I'd produced that was an unmitigated disaster both creatively and financially. It should never have been made. I made the decision to move ahead without the funds in place.

At first I was cavalier about it. I just assumed that I'd always be able to find a solution as I had in the past and clean up the mess and this time would be not different.

However, this time we were on the receiving end of rather unscrupulous individuals who saw us coming a mile away. If you saw the movie "*The Sting*", well, we got stung.

After paying a lawyer in New York City, he kept reassuring us we could begin production. We hired a crew of over 100 people. We began production.

The promised money we paid for never materialized and thus begun the most dramatic, debilitating period of my life. It's taken me over twenty-five years to clean up that wreckage from my past. There were people who really did hope I would find myself shuffling off my mortal coil sooner than later and meeting the source of all-evil in a very fiery pit of hot, burning coals, fire and whatever horrible suffering I would endure.

In retrospect, I can't say I blame them. In truth, I've reached out to as many of them as I can and wherever possible I've tried to make personal or financial amends. And I learned to forgive the offending lawyer for being less than forthright.

Here's what is interesting about that experience. I've never done it again. Even though I'm in the midst of a very trying time as a result of my brain injury, I am extremely proactive in reaching out to my creditors and shareholders, and letting them know where I am and what I am doing. There is one with whom my contact is minimal. But, that's another story.

Equally important is the fact I pray every day that if there is anyone I have hurt financially, spiritually, or emotionally that they be able to forgive me.

I did a lot of crazy things when I was a young man. Things I can't even imagine doing today. But, I know I've hurt people – not intentionally, but through my misguided behaviour.

What I've tried to do is give people the space to be able to tell me just how angry they are or how hurt they were. And, I'm very clear about boundaries. I have no issue with anyone saying, "I think you were a selfish, self-centered jerk", (or expletive) and they can say it once. But, there is no room for abuse. Once is enough.

What I tell them ahead of meeting them is if they wish to be abusive, or in any way violent, that is where I draw the line. I don't do abuse. And there is a significant difference between an honest communication and abusive behaviour.

I find that when I am cleaning up relationships it is very important to let the person know, "I hear how angry you are. I can see that I've hurt you a great deal. I am truly sorry for that, and I'm willing to go to any lengths to repair our relationship, including never contacting you again if that is what you want."

For some people, that may be the kindest thing we can do as seeing us just brings up too many painful memories for them. In my own case, that's not been the outcome.

In some cases such as my Dad's, I had to go to his grave. My father hurt me a great deal as a child. I don't need to go into the specifics here, but it traumatized me, and left me incredibly damaged and has taken a lifetime to heal.

What I did is I visited the town where he was born and is buried. I stood at his grave and told him how much pain he had caused me and then I told him I forgave him and wished his soul peace and acceptance. I now realize just how troubled he was, dying alone, with none of us around him. We reap what we sow.

A great deal of emotion washed over me, and I just stood there as tears flowed down my face. At last I could let my dad go. I told him I loved him, and I'm sure he loved me too, even though he never uttered those words to me as a child.

When I'm speaking or teaching in my class, I've often said, "it's incredible how hard I am on myself. If anyone ever did to me what I do to myself, I'd charge him or her with assault and battery.

So many of us are just so hard on ourselves. It is really important to learn to forgive ourselves and just learn to lighten up and accept ourselves, warts and all.

If people would be totally honest, even those who seem to have exemplary lives will admit that they often berate themselves for simple mistakes. We all need forgiveness. It's imperative for our mental wellbeing.

I am grateful today to say that while the young man and his family may need to take responsibility for his actions, I have totally forgiven him on a spiritual level and I do pray for their well being almost every day.

–Chapter Ten–

I Ask

STEP 6. I ASK
I make known my specific requests, asking my partner's support in knowing that the Master Mind is fulfilling my needs. (Make your request now: "I request ____"

GROUP RESPONSE: "I know the Master Mind has heard you and is providing you with what you have asked for."

Talk about one of the most confusing parts of this whole process. One of my big problems is that my mind (faulty filter) starts chatting to me especially around five in the morning when I come to after a night's sleep. Sitting on the end of my bed is the little guy whom I mentioned earlier and resides in my head and he just smiles at me with that Oh I know something you don't! Then he starts up, *"It's not okay to ask God for something because you don't deserve it. How selfish can you be when millions are starving to death? You know money is the root of all evil!"*

Those thoughts spin endlessly in a repetitive loop like a rotisserie in my mind. They are interspersed with *"You are not worthy. Who do you think you are? What a lot of nonsense. Do you really think God is up there like a short order cook waiting to fill your order?"* Then my inner voice kicks in and responds to the previous thoughts, "I don't know, maybe?"

However, when we look at scripture there really is a lot of *"Ask you and will receive, seek and you will find, knock, and it will be opened to you."*

On that theme, as far as money being evil, it's inanimate. It is just something we exchange for goods and services. The "love of money is the root of all evil." When I will sell out my integrity, be blatantly dishonest or just enrich myself at the expense of someone else, I am headed for big trouble.

I have been in two Master Mind groups over the past 15 years. My first one ended when I left Toronto and moved to eastern Ontario in 2001.

When my second Master Mind group began, I was in the business of just asking for financial help. Over a period of years, we had a lawyer, a former member of the Royal Canadian Mounted Police and then a former military officer. That group eventually came down to just three of us: Richard, Bill, who was an avowed agnostic and retired psychiatrist and I. The three of us held over 600 meetings over a six or seven year period. It was Bill who got us to start to examine the concept of asking for humility and clarity of thought.

At first my mind railed against this idea. I kept asking for financial help. With Bill's influence I began to shift my emphasis and ask for help with my business, my finances, my relationship with my then wife Deb and my children Brendan and Laurel (who were teenagers at the time) and my children from my first marriage Andrew & Colleen. Slowly I began to come around to Bill's way of thinking. I can remember saying for the first time, " Okay, please guide me to peace of mind and humility."

I was expecting that I would have to drop to my knees right there in the restaurant or join the Salvation Army. I actually saw humility – let me correct that statement – I *perceived* humility as a fatal flaw, a weakness. Once again, here I was at the mercy of my faulty filter and misinformation from my childhood.

I never recognized that humility was something worth pursuing in itself. I never imagined it could be the key to true happiness and serenity. I'm not suggesting for one moment that I have it, but today I really see the value in seeking it, as it provides so many benefits when I choose to ask for it in my everyday life.

Originally I held the attitude that people would walk all over me if I were humble. I confused humility with humiliation. I know the difference from the perspective of syntax and semantics, but not in terms of emotions.

Still, when I looked around, whom did I really admire? My friend Bill for one! In spite of his extensive medical knowledge, and his numerous degrees including a specialty in anesthesiology, he never talked about his training or made a big deal of it. He was just a very, very humble man.

I came to have a tremendous amount of love and respect for him. My friend Richard was the same way. In fact, most of the people I really like and admire are exactly the same way. If anyone were the odd man out, it was I when I really think about it.

Learning what to ask and pray for was a big part of the journey for me. Getting through the thought that I was worthy of any kind of Higher Power or God's love was also another hurdle, which I had to overcome. It is amazing to me how many of us have been so dramatically effected by our upbringings. Not that anyone recognized or acknowledged it back then. It's just the way things were, especially if you were to view my family from the outside. We lived in a very beautiful home, and my father had been a civic politician and a successful insurance executive. It didn't fit my picture of what alcoholism and violence looked like.

Coming to a place of acceptance that there was a Power in the first place, (who was not like my own father), then accepting the idea that this Power could be personal to me and that this same Higher Power could and would help me if I asked Him/Her/It too, was a very radical idea. As I said earlier, if you already have a traditional faith, you are that much further ahead of where I am.

I began with very simple requests. "Can I receive one million dollars or two million dollars?" That didn't work too well. "Can you please guide me to the best possible result with my creditors?" That worked. "Can you please guide me to the best possible result with a project, so the greatest good is produced for all involved? " That worked. "Can you please guide me to financial solvency?" That worked. "Can you please guide me to peace of mind, humility and clarity of thought?" Wow, that really started to kick in.

Then slowly I began to see and understand that there were many areas of my life where I really needed guidance. I was dumbfounded by the turn of events 14 months ago that have led up to today whereby not one of the 312 projects we pitched were approved.

You see, there I was thinking, "Okay, I can control this. I can fix this if I just put my mind to it." No, I can't! This was the beginning of the understanding that the brain injury had impacted me in ways I couldn't have comprehended.

I kept thinking I've always been able to overcome every obstacle in my past. Surely I can overcome this! This is the specific discovery that drove me 14 months ago to really begin the process of surrendering. After almost 42 years of seeking a spiritual practice, I was still trying to run the show myself.

As far as my spiritual life was concerned I was now willing to turn it over. When it came to my career, money or romantic relationships, hold on there God, I can handle those. If you can only please guide me to the success I've been asking for, all will be well.

In retrospect, if I had kept going I would have continued to see the same results. All I would have ended up doing was wasting the money I had in reserve while trying to get yet another production going. When I earnestly began to seek a Higher Power's guidance, it really started to produce results. Big results like the overwhelming "NO!"

That was difficult to comprehend. I have, or had, a very simplistic view of God. In fact, it was very immature. I know that Scripture also talks about having the faith of a child. I had the magical thinking of a child. Apparently Steve Jobs had it too, and it essentially killed him because he thought he could overcome his cancer through very basic and child like beliefs – just meditate, eat vegan, stay away from meat.

Not one of those things in themselves is bad, though, in my opinion, they are not a replacement for science or modern medicine. In retrospect, he would have been better served with a combination of both disciplines.

In my own case, I have to let go of this kind of thinking that just because I'm doing everything correctly, the results are always going to go my way. If I'm really seeking spiritual guidance, I have to be ready to accept 'no' as an answer also. Perhaps a better prayer is "thy will be done".

The interesting thing is that when I did the Canfield Coaching, I had come to realize I've had an incredible number of things work out. Far more yes than no's.

I've not been exactly hard done by. It was only through looking at my life with a new lens that I began to see all the wonderful accomplishments I've been able to achieve. For example being an award-winning professor and working with amazing people like John Munro and Vicki Keith (the world record holder in marathon swimming) in assisting them to make *Penguins Can Fly*, a film about children with special needs. It played in Los Angeles for Academy Award consideration and helped raise a significant amount of money for the various YMCA's that have programs for kids with both physical and intellectual disabilities. It has been an incredible privilege to be the author of a book. I've had the pleasure of speaking to a significant number of people over the years about overcoming adversity. All these events have been extremely positive and have led to a real sense of gratitude and accomplishment.

As a result of this realization, I've come to another conclusion. I don't know what is good for me or anyone else a great deal of the time. My mind says, "Of course you know." But I really don't.

Letting Go and Letting The Master Mind

What I'm learning through the process of letting go of my business and possibly my career is that there may be something I am much better suited for. I will look at the possibilities of teaching and writing non-fiction books as well as inspirational and motivational speaking. I may continue to pursue writing and producing film and television. Or, it may be a combination of all of the above. As they say, "when one door closes another opens."

What can I ask my Master Mind Partners for? Anything you want, with this caveat: "If what I have asked for is not what is best for me, please send me what I need instead of what I want."

Having goals as well as having a plan for your life and, asking for guidance, is paramount to finding yours heart's desire.

I've known all my life that I really want to share with others what I've learned along the way. But, I was such a nonconformist in my earlier years that my mind (faulty filter) still says, "Dave, you are too much of a rebel for mainstream society to embrace". In fact, I've discovered that I am incredibly conservative with liberal leanings.

I am so grateful to say that these past three weeks I've felt a conscious contact with The Divine that I've never felt before. Getting here to West Vancouver fulfills a dream I've had for years. It has been so wonderful. I had a vision of an apartment with a view of what I was looking for, only it was up a little higher up the mountain. Then I made the decision a few months ago if I move here, I want to be closer to the two small towns that make up West Vancouver, Ambleside and Dundarave. I want to ride my bike and go for walks and not have to get in my car all the time. I'm finally getting sick of driving to go anywhere. One of the downsides of living in the country is you have to drive everywhere.

I did ask for guidance about seeking this teaching job at the university, about selling my house, moving out of two places with only 5 days notice. The fact that I was able to deal with my Toronto apartment and rent out my house in the country was a miracle in itself. I'm astounded at how it all just came together with so many kind people pitching in to give me a hand.

Admittedly, one of the most difficult things for me to do is ask anyone for help. I am always happy to help others if I can, but there is some quirk in me that I struggle with asking others for the same. It's not healthy for them or me, as I rob people of the opportunity to feel good by being able to be of service.

I did originally ask the Master Mind for help. To keep my production company functioning, I worked as hard as I ever had in my entire career. I don't know how I could have worked any harder, smarter or more diligently. In the end, I was left with either gaining acceptance of the result or getting angry and resentful.

I had to accept that I have an injury. Mine is a very specific injury that affects my selling ability. I seem to be okay writing this as I'm relating to my own experience. This I can do. And it is very therapeutic writing it. So, there is a very specific emotional benefit to it.

No is Also An Answer

"We don't always get what we "ask for" is another lesson I've learned and "No is also an answer." It may be that I can't see why it would be "no" at the time, or it might seem grossly unfair to me, but if I look back on my life and honestly examine the result of some of the most difficult periods I've ever had, then I see why in retrospect I had to feel that disappointment. As I said before, I've never learned anything on a good day.

Yes Does Happen Too

Yes, happens too. I did ask for a teaching position and it did come up almost miraculously. I did ask to live where I am right now. And they're both literally what I had hoped for. You could never have predicted either one of those outcomes a short while ago. All of the shows that we did produce were stellar in both their ratings or creatively. I've been praying for a deeper more meaningful relationship with the Higher Power of my understanding. That seems to be manifesting.

I've also asked my Master Mind Group to help me achieve with written goals and find peace of mind and humility. And, here I am working away on a beautiful sunny and warm Friday afternoon in West Vancouver.

I'm asking The Master Mind to guide me to the best possible outcome, and the best results I can produce today in every area of my life.

Only time will tell if these results match my others. However, I don't suggest going out and nearly getting beat to death like I did to discover a new way to live. There are smarter ways to do this, but it appears that this experience was to be part of my journey.

I've asked two of my friends about forming a Master Mind group here. It has already been eight weeks since I left Ontario and the only thing I really miss besides my children and friends are my Master Mind connections. I've phoned both Richard and Bruce on a few occasions and spoken to Will once. I'm keeping the connection alive.

I am also praying more now than I ever have, and I am sincerely seeking guidance. My friend and accountant out here, Mike, whom I've known for over 30 years has given me a series of Unity lectures that I'm finding very helpful. One thing about being on my own much of the time is I have a lot of time to meditate and think about life. I've done all those things in spades recently.

It is important for me, or anyone else, to have the support of fellow travelers. The question I would ask myself is, if I had to leave the planet tonight, would I be satisfied with my life so far? My answer is that I would be grateful for all the blessings I've had. Has my life been perfect? No, but, it's been very, very good, and I've been very blessed.

I am human and thus imperfect, so my mind quickly forgets all that when I don't get what I want. Have I mentioned my chronic infantile omnipotence? My late friend Jack

Humphrey gave me that expression and I love it. That's when you don't get what you want you lay on the floor and flail away. Acceptable at age one year, irritating at age 2 years, downright rude as a young man or woman and just plain embarrassing as an adult. But guess what? I still get bouts of it.

I think if we keep asking for guidance and have a sincere desire in our hearts to change and be of service, then I suspect we will find ourselves in a much better place than if it is only material possessions we seek.

I don't necessarily want to downplay material achievements either. I would still like to be financially self supporting and able to live a comfortable lifestyle. At some point I would like to be able to spend a few weeks or a month per year in a warm climate during the worst of the rainy season here. I would still like to continue to have nice cars and money to maintain them. I want to be able to eat healthy and buy the nutritious food and vitamins that I need to maintain my health.

I want to continue to belong to the West Vancouver Fitness and Aquatic Center where I was this morning. I want to be able to go out once a week to a show or a movie and have dinner out a few nights a week. If I am fortunate enough to meet someone wonderful, I would always like to be able to enjoy treating her to a nice holiday or a road trip.

One of the things I did today was to examine my finances. I spoke to the payroll department of the university, where I'm teaching. I am only teaching ten hours per week, and I now know what my net income per month will be for the next four months, (the length of my contract.) I have no guarantee that the contract will be renewed.

I will have to cash in some of my retirement investments, unless my house sells. I have asked the Divine Intelligence to guide me to my greatest good in this area, and I will call Richard and Bruce to ask them if they can pray for me too. I will arrange to meet with accountant Mike and perhaps one other friend, and do a review of what my options are. Some business guidance would be helpful.

While I feel nervous about it, I'm not panicked. I really do think that I'm going to be guided to the best outcome. I've been marking the first 50 or 60 papers for my new students. I have my lecture prepared for Wednesday and Thursday of this week. I'm ahead of the curve on being organized. The critical thing is that these four months are giving me the chance to take stock of my life and reprioritize what it is that I want to do. I can then create a plan to achieve those goals.

I've responded to one of the insurance companies that are handling my disability claim. I have followed through with a number of calls and emails.

This morning I prayed and asked to be the most productive that I can be. I've broken my day down into manageable chunks. I don't have to take on all my issues at once. As an example, last Friday I wrote to the President of Wells Fargo Bank in San Francisco because no one in the bank has any experience with someone like me coming to them ahead of every going in default and asking them to stop payments and interest while I resolve my pending legal case.

All I can do is be rigorously honest with them. I sent the proposal and letter out to them a few weeks ago, and I have not heard anything back yet. I will let you know how it goes. After all, he is the President of one the largest banks in the United States, dealing in billions of dollars. I'm sure he's got a few more important things on his plate than Dave Brady's letter about a modest line of credit. It turns out I've paid about 125% of what I had originally borrowed in interest payments alone over the past four years because I've been fundamentally unconscious about these matters since my injury.

> October 4th, I've spoken to Executive office at Wells Fargo, and it would appear they're not able to do anything and I've asked the young man I spoke to, to speak to someone on my behalf at an executive level.
>
> None of the folks I'm talking to have any authority to make an actual decision except say "no."

From a corporate communications point of view it is interesting to see how different corporate cultures function. Two years ago I had a problem with United Airlines. I was flying my crew on Super Volcano and contacted the President's office. Not only did he respond within a day, but also his staff cleared up the problem for me that day. Today I share that positive story with as many people as I can. There is no doubt in my mind about the success of the new United Airlines or what a powerful example Jeff Smisek is as a CEO. He genuinely seems to care. I'd like to hope that John Stumpf is the same kind of person.

Today is January 28, 2014. I just received a very nice letter from Wells Fargo Bank. They have declined my request to put my payments on hold while I resolve my financial issues with the insurance company. I don't believe the CEO was ever made aware of my situation. I did propose that the Bank look at purchasing bulk copies of this book and I would be happy to come down and speak to some of their clients on the challenges associated with aging and overcoming adversity. They acknowledged that all my payments were up to date.

To their credit, they are open to the idea of looking at my book and have requested a copy of it when it is finished. I am grateful it does keep the door open and at some point I hope to speak to the CEO in person and I will mention this experience to him. I looked him up online and see that like me; he grew up in the northern US, near the border with Canada and seems like a very decent guy.

One of the challenges I've always had is I want things "NOW". If I pray and ask my Master Mind group for something today, I'm hoping I'll have the answer tomorrow, or the next day, at worse.

If I could speak to God in person, I'd have to say, "What's with your time line?" Boy, you can be slow. Okay, there are over seven billion people all pleading, crying, asking "Help me, guide me, save me, save this member of my family, heal whomever, get that rotten bastard over there – oops" and I forget that like the banker, God may be a tad busy. I'm not actually sure that God Himself/Herself/Itself actually sits around figuring out who to save, fix, heal, reward, punish, chastise, pat on the back or kick in the ass as we do have free will. The point is I think most of us do a very good job of doing all those nasty things to ourselves. I suspect poor old God just sits there in a state of amazement at how hard we are on ourselves.

As I grow in humility and acquire a conscious contact through prayer and meditation, I'm led to the understanding that I am able to access the Divine Spark, which is the living presence of the Divine Intelligence within me. Or, I have within me the power that has emerged from the universe since its inception, that is, the consciousness of this Power. And that is what I am coming to believe. We all have within us this Divine spark that if we are attuned to Divine Grace, we can find solutions that would baffle others. We are able to deal with pain and calamity in a way that others are not able to. We are able to enjoy life and feel good about all of our experiences, both positive and negative, and we see the real value in experiencing them as a necessary part of our growth.

It is important to keep asking our Master Mind partners for guidance until we know that we have the right answer. Once again, we may have to pray for acceptance of the way things are. Especially if what we've asked for does not appear.

I just glanced out the window and the late afternoon sun is highlighting the clouds over Vancouver Island, and there are no words to describe just how beautiful it is, cloudy or not. There are about a half dozen large ocean going container ships anchored in the harbor off Point Grey. Thank you God for the beauty of this world.

The Greatest Answered Prayer of My Life

I want to end this chapter with perhaps the most important ask and prayer I ever uttered in my entire life, outside of the day in New York City when I got down on my knees in Saint Patrick's Cathedral and asked, "If there is a God, please help me". At that moment all of my cravings for mood altering substances were removed from my life and have never returned. It occurred the day my youngest daughter Laurel was born.

Laurel, who was probably one of the youngest premature babies ever to survive when she was born, only weighted 880 grams (less than two pounds); her little torso fit in the palm of my hand, where she slept for the first three nights of her life, because I didn't want to let go of her. I remember going into a bathroom at St. Joseph's Hospital in London Ontario, getting down on my knees, and sobbing uncontrollably, begging God to spare her. My own mother, who had been at Sick Children's Hospital for the latter part of her nursing career, told me not to get my hopes up.

The doctors warned us of the potential pitfalls that lay ahead as they had no experience with such a small baby in 1989. Laurel's bilirubin was so high they had to exchange all of her blood within 48 hours of her birth. She had to be intubated and they warned us because her lungs had not matured that there could be ventricle hemorrhaging (brain bleeding), which could cause unknown learning disabilities or the potential loss or impairment of her eyesight, as well as other physical maladies. Then we had to cope with her heart stopping randomly over the first few weeks of her life. She was having cardiac events called bradycardias, where her heart would stop and we would have to take her little feet and tickle them so her heart would start up again. She had so many tubes in her it was just so painful to watch it all unfolding.

When I think back now and look at Laurel today, beautiful, incredibly intelligent, the most amazing blue eyes you've ever seen, a real fighter who is just such a remarkable young woman, I am filled with gratitude. In spite of their dire warnings, she has successfully completed her university degree with honors, has just received her first paying position as a speaker, and has already launched a new play she's written and will star in with her brother Brendan, directing.

I'm amazed. That ask was perhaps the most important prayer of my life and I am so grateful that it was answered in the affirmative, I probably should not complain ever again if not another request is answered.

–Chapter Eleven–

I Give Thanks

STEP 7. I GIVE THANKS
I give thanks that the Master Mind is responding to my needs and I assume the same feelings I would have if my requests were fulfilled.

It is a well-known fact that our minds cannot differentiate between the perceived and the actual circumstances in our lives. In other words, if we speak out loud and affirm, *"I am grateful today that the Master Mind is guiding me to peace of mind, prosperity, real joy in my life and the best possible outcome in all my affairs",* our Master Mind begins to work to bring about the very results that we are giving thanks for.

If we want more in our life, we give thanks for what we have. When I was in the thick of my recent challenges, what did I do? I had to pray and meditate to ensure that I didn't focus on what I wasn't getting. When I did break down and worry, which I did from time to time because none of us is perfect, I was praying for what I didn't want. I'm not talking about healthy caution and concern about our wellbeing. What I'm talking about is repetitive, compulsive worry; the kind of worrying that robs us of peace of mind and harms the relationships we have with those closest to us.

When we give thanks for the simple things in life, we open the floodgate of blessings. We begin attracting to us those things we desire having. If we have good health, we give thanks.

I have a gratitude list in the front of my daily journal, which I read every morning. Included in it are my children, my brothers and sisters, my nieces and nephews, my past career successes, my nice new apartment in West Vancouver, my new teaching position, my friends, all the good things I have in my life now, and all I have been given. This helps keep me in a state of grace.

When we begin giving thanks for the entire blessing we've been given, and when we share with others what we have been given, we also open ourselves up for a lot of good to come into our lives. There is an old saying, "If you want to keep what you have, give it away."

In other words, if something is working for you and you feel a real sense of gratitude for it, share it with others. It can be as simple as swimming two or three days a week, and then telling others you care about how good you feel and the obvious physical benefits of exercise. It won't matter if they take you up on your offer to swim with them. Just trying to be of service opens you up for more benefits.

Tithing is the same way with respect to money, and it is something I wish I would do, especially when I'm worried about money.

When we make the decision to imagine how we would feel if we actually received what our heart's desire is, then we open up a magical channel straight to the source of all things in the universe. It's why creative people and inventors are able to step out in faith and have amazing results come to pass in their lives. They experience the very thing we're examining here. On many occasions, they will often appear to have failed, but to these remarkable individuals it is just a temporary setback. Thomas Edison said, "I have not failed. I've just found 10,000 ways that won't work."

Once again the New Testament provides us with evidence from the Gospels, and I'm sure there will also be a similar writing in the Torah or other religious texts. In Mark 11:22-24 "Whatever you ask in prayer, believe that you have received it, and it will be done for you."

Now I suspect there must be some common sense caveats attached to this. One, you must believe in something greater than you are. Two, you can't be asking for anything that would harm anyone. Three, you can't have "wrong motives", like asking to have buddy down the road drop dead because you covet his wife, or if you are buddy's wife, you can't be coveting Fred next door because he's more successful than your husband.

I believe the point is that if we have a strong belief in a Power greater than ourselves, if we practice prayer and meditation, and if we are truly seeking to increase our awareness of the Master Mind's will in our lives, and we want to be of service to others, then we will increase our chances exponentially of attracting to us what we really desire.

The great thing too about having a Master Mind Group is that we have a sounding board for many of our requests. It also helps us in the process of coming to believe that our requests are being answered.

Affirmations really work. It is an interesting experiment to step out in faith and believe that you already possess that which you ask for. There is a law of attraction and I do believe this is one of the keys to it. I believe that is why both the book and film, *The Secret*, were so successful.

There are numerous books on Success Principles including Jack Canfield's, which is really just an extrapolation on the work of Napoleon Hill. However, all books, including a wonderful book by Catherine Ponder, *Open Your Mind to Prosperity*, all say the same thing.

It really does work if we allow ourselves to reinforce our belief by affirming "I am receiving", and then add what it is you are wishing to attain. If we affirm it out loud, we can often feel a chill go through us, which seems to me to be a sort of conscious contact with the 'source' of all abundance, peace and knowledge.

How do we know if the Master Mind is responding to our needs? Often, as was the case of my recent university appointment, the thought popped into my head to check that specific university, as I was in the process of meditating.

I had mentioned to my Master Mind group that I need a change. Something had to give as I'd gone through the previously mentioned hundreds of "no's" on my new film and television projects.

It was effortless. When I looked online that day, I saw the advertisement for the position. I had less than 48 hours in which to submit my application.

Prior to that, I was praying, writing and just hammering as hard as I could to close a deal. I was so focused on closing and creating new projects that I couldn't see that the answer over and over was no. I believe I was on the verge of causing myself serious physical harm with stress and worry because of the incessant number of no's I was receiving.

It was also beginning to affect my self-esteem. I was not feeling good about myself. I was grappling emotionally trying to accept that what I had in the past was gone - as far as some of my creative gifts were concerned. I also didn't know if this injury has left me permanently disabled, or if it is something temporary.

However, I didn't stop asking for guidance and help. I've never really been able to accept defeat in the past. Especially in this case, as I had to give up a business that I had only started up 3 years before. Prior to this unfortunate event, we were headed on a straight trajectory towards all the success I'd ever hoped for.

Unanswered Prayer

This raises one of the questions that have plagued me my entire life. If God or the Master Mind does hear us, why does He/It not answer all prayers? How do we explain the horrors of Lake Megantic, the Tsunami in Asia a few years ago, or the World Trade Center? Did many of them not pray and believe they would be helped?

This is the paradox of faith. I admit that I have a limited understanding of the universe. I don't know what the Master Mind's will is for any of us as I indicated earlier. I do know that these events seem to occur randomly and are beyond my comprehension. What is also inconceivable to me is why any of us must sometimes suffer so much pain and horror before death. It doesn't make any sense to me at all.

I know that we all have to face death, and for many of us it will be sooner rather than later. That begs the question, "What does lie on the other side?" What is the point of suffering with terminal illness? Why do people suffer so much in this life? Why do innocent people die in tragic accidents?"

I don't know. I really don't. And, it was the argument that the British atheist Christopher Hitchens in his book, *God is Not Great* posed. His case intrigued me. Here was a man who was clearly way smarter than I was. Nonetheless, I started to dig into his story. I would discover that according to certain reports, he died an active alcoholic and that according to rumor from people close to the family his mother had committed suicide as a result of an affair with a Church of England minister.

Suddenly I can see why he would have the feeling that God is not Great! He was such a brilliant writer and an incredibly dedicated human being. I would have enjoyed speaking with him.

When I was a young man and working with a number of left-leaning folks, I too was an avowed agnostic. I could never have the absolute faith of an atheist. Now I have seen evidence, irrefutable evidence, that often when we do pray and ask for guidance and help, we get it.

Master Mind Groups

Many of us had Master Mind groups, perhaps without knowing it if we were involved in any kind of spiritual or philosophical movements. There were also the human potential movements of the 70s, such as EST, of which I was a big fan. I did the training, the six-day, the workshops and in essence, many of these seminars and workshops would set up the dynamic that would further inspire me to pursue what I've come to know today as Master Mind movement.

Is it new? Not really. It was Christ who said, "For where two or three gather in my name, there am I with them." Now, I'm not even a traditional Christian at this stage of my life. But I believe that the Master Mind or Divine intelligence is there and available to all of us if we just ask. There seems to be some universal Intelligence, Divine spirit, and an undeniable force at work throughout the universe that when we ask for help, we seem to get it.

For many, it is God who is the Master Mind. I'm more inclined to accept the concept of Mother/Father God or the Holy Spirit. I'm also not too worried whether or not He/It is going to fry my derriere when I get to the other side because I had doubts. And if you are one of the ones who think he is, then I humbly ask you to pray for me. Only time will tell which one of us is correct. I'm willing to bet my life on it, I've already been to hell. It holds no sway over me. As the old saying goes, "Religion is for those afraid of going to hell, spirituality, which I am an advocate of, is for those of us who've already been there."

Obviously, it is up to you. I believe the Master Mind likes me just as I am. So, I will continue to look at my list and continue to add to it

The Lesson

In spite of my difficulties, I did give thanks. I did imagine myself sitting in this very chair writing, looking at the same view I am currently enjoying.

I do believe my life is taking a turn for the better. I have to adjust to so much in my life.

However, I believe it will only be temporary. I will be able to get this book published. It will open doors for me to be of service through seminars and online webinars where I can personally share my journey with you.

If I can overcome a debilitating brain injury, wind down my company (or turn it over to Mike, my son and Tony) let go of old ideas about myself and others and notions of what success are, and just be grateful for what I have today, I am going to be all right.

–Chapter Twelve–

I Dedicate My Life

STEP 8. I DEDICATE MY LIFE
I now have a covenant in which it is agreed that the Master Mind is supplying me with an abundance of all things necessary to live a successful and happy life.

I dedicate myself to be of maximum service to God and those around me; to live in a manner that sets the highest example for others to follow; and to remain responsive to God's guidance.

I go forth with a spirit of enthusiasm, excitement and expectancy. I am at peace.

As I sit here, the sky is almost mystical. I've never seen anything like it. The clouds are hanging layer upon layer over Point Grey, and the setting sun is reflecting off of them. They are a wonderful shade of grey and white with a tinge of pink. It was supposed to be raining today and instead it has turned into a gorgeous first day of fall.

At this stage of my life, I no longer find myself limited to any specific theology or traditional formal religion. I may in the future. I've recently returned to two non-denominational Christian churches. One is called The Sutherland Church in North Vancouver where the minister there is Todd Weibe. He is a very unusual and bright young man who has an incredibly open mind. I'm glad I've met him and his friends. The other is Unity Spiritual Center in Vancouver. I am very comfortable at both of them.

I sincerely believe that all these churches and faiths contain the answer to the big questions about faith and what it is we should really be seeking in our lives. They also help me connect to a community of like-minded people. The older I get the more I see how important this is for our emotional and spiritual well-being.

There is a wonderful book, *Thank God For Evolution* by Michael Dowd that allows us to see just how it is that we all got to where we are and why. For so many of us, we are plagued by feelings of guilt, shame, blame and a sense of failure as we look back on our lives. There is no need to be.

As stated in the opening, the purpose of my book is to guide you through the process of getting the most you can out of either your middle age or "golden years" (as they are euphemistically called), find real peace of mind, happiness and prosperity regardless of your current circumstances.

Your life can't be that much more precarious than mine is at the moment, unless and heaven forbid, you've been diagnosed with a terminal illness. I can't compete with that. You may be one of those blessed people, whose financial lives are on a rock solid foundation, thus removing one of the greatest stressors in life. However, you may be one of those aching inside trying to understand how it is you got to this point having done everything right, but your life feels so wrong or incomplete.

I've spent the first two-thirds of my life getting. I would like to spend the last one-third giving. As the Good Book says, and I paraphrase, "it is better to give than receive."

I have devoted much of my life to the pursuit of spiritual principles. Here is what I believe today. There is a God and it's not me. I like to think of Mother/Father God.

On a practical level, how can we utilize this step in our daily lives? As an example, I called my insurance company today to report my cracked windshield, which was damaged on the drive here via the United States. They've arranged for me to take my car in tomorrow to get it replaced. However, I have a Mercedes B200 Turbo. This car is not available in the United States, only in Europe and Canada. The first challenge with this car is that the windshield, which must to be replaced, can be one of three versions: One is standard glass, one is for automatic rain sensors, and the third is both rain-sensitive and light-sensitive. I found out I mine is the second type. I am very grateful for my great insurance coverage, which has zero deductible.

My next challenge is that my Turbo Charger is not working properly. These can be very expensive parts or systems to repair, so I asked some friends about it. They gave me the name of a good Mercedes mechanic under the Oak

Street Bridge, who can hopefully repair the turbo charger. Then everything in my life will be repaired. I just ask and believe that I am being supplied even at this mundane level of having to get my car fixed and that I'm led to the right people. Let's see what happens.

How To Tell If Your Life Is Working

If you want to get a sense of how your life is working, glance around and see how many things need to be repaired in your life. How are your shoes? What kind of shape is your home in? Is it neat and tidy or filled with garbage or cluttered? How is your car? Is the engine light on? Mine is. I've had it checked, but my garage in Ontario had no experience with this problem, so I've found someone that hopefully will be able to repair it at a reasonable cost. I like my car. It is a really nice automobile that affords me safety and great quality.

The Spirit of Enthusiasm is Alive and Well

Well, here it is Tuesday September 24th. I've come back from my new mechanic's, and he was kind enough to arrange for a rental car for me. Hans is German and has worked on Mercedes Benz's since 1965. I like that. He's one of us – a "boomer". What is interesting is how people, unrelated to him, were so quick to give him a wonderful endorsement as someone who offered honest and great work.

I also received word today from one of the major insurance companies that two of my claims have been approved because I stopped working. At present, I'm still no longer able to work as the creator of television shows and movies. So far so good! This covenant seems to be working.

Last week I did an online seminar with a young man in the United States who is involved in the world of book publicity and marketing. He has helped a great number of best-selling authors get publicity for their books. As I suspected, he also pointed out that the best area to focus on in order to be of maximum service, is to offer seminars, workshops and weekend trainings.

I now have confirmation that I'm headed in the right direction. I want to transform my life, let go of worry and either heal from my physical disability, or find a new way to compensate for it.

I am really grateful for my automobile insurance company, TD Meloche Monnex. They are amazing because they really care.

I am also very grateful for the two insurance companies that cover my bank loans and lines of credit. They just stepped up to the plate after the forms were sent in and I explained my situation to them. Canada Life and Bankers Insurance of Florida have been exemplary. Again, since I made the decision to turn my will and life over and use the Eight Steps and specifically this step, I am being supplied with all the things that are necessary for me to live my life today.

What is amazing to me is how I am being supplied with what I need in order to survive. Yes, I am having to utilize my savings, but I have savings. Those savings were a direct result of turning my will and life over to the care of the Master Mind, some years ago and asking for help.

It is so interesting to me since that very black day back at the end of July when I decided to close my business down. I was despondent and it felt like my life was ending. It was like a death to me. The sorrow was overwhelming as were the endless rejections. What a time that was. I am so grateful for my friends. If you don't have friends at this stage of your life, you need to make some very, very quickly. They are out there waiting to talk to you too, especially if you carry a positive message.

A Master Mind Group will create the environment for you to have a covenant that you can believe in. You really do have to believe that you can be guided to your greatest good, regardless of what your current financial or emotional circumstances are today. Believe me, they will change. We can't give up one day too soon. I have just experienced this in spades.

One of my early problems (and probably why I wasted so many years) was I wouldn't enter into a covenant with the Master Mind about anything except for drinking. I believe I mentioned earlier when it came to relationships my attitude was, "Hold on, I'll handle that if you don't mind. Business. Whoa! This is my territory." Well, not anymore.

The Gift of Families

I'm so grateful that I did ask for help from my family. My youngest daughter recently told me "We won the Dad lottery with you." I just got goose bumps writing this. It was so nice to hear.

Overcoming Adversity

A year ago this past July, I made the decision to surrender my life completely to the care and guidance of my Higher Power. I had no idea it would lead me here today. At that point in my life, I was in the midst of editing three shows, and we were on fire creatively. However, the shows we were finishing were started right around the time of the assault. For the better part of that year after we delivered the completed shows every single pitch we did was rejected.

Words cannot express how depressing and difficult it was to experience that kind of disappointment because I honestly believed the ideas were good ones, and only time will tell if I was correct.

I was left in a state of real despair and hopelessness. I never thought I would feel normal again. I never thought I would be happy or have any degree of peace in my life.

Yet here I am sixteen months after making that fateful decision to trust in a Higher Power completely, and the ship is turning around. Not as David Brady Productions, which is on life support, but as David Brady, author, lecturer, seminar leader and speaker. I feel that this step is working and that my covenant with my Master Mind is coming true, and I am being supplied with an abundance of all I need to live my life.

As a result of this reinvention of myself, I'm actually feeling peaceful, which is really hard to believe. "Peaceful" is not how I would have described myself a few months ago. Not even a few weeks ago.

Today, I have enough. I have enough money for my current payables. I have enough emotional stability to let go of fear, worry and resentment (most of the time).

I am off to a faculty meeting this afternoon at 4:45. I had a goal to finish this book by September 30th (editorial note: today it is February 13, 2014, as I finish editing this).

While it's not going to be complete, as far as a rewrite or editing goes, I'm getting very close to the end.

I actually feel excitement again. And I really thought all of that had gone from my life. I had a good conversation with my buddy Bruce yesterday. He's fighting the good fight with MS. He hopes to come out from Ontario and visit me, and I'm looking forward to that. He's going to travel with a young lady or two who will help him out of his wheelchair. They are friends of ours.

I have enough food in my fridge to eat healthy and balanced meals. I get pretty tired of my own cooking or not cooking. My friends would burst out laughing at my referencing cooking when it seems that all I eat is fresh fruit and salads with nuts, skim milk (okay with cocoa in it) and really plain chicken, steak or potatoes. I actually think it's my lack of culinary horizons that have caused me the loss of my real true romances in life.

One of the big concerns I have at this moment is the sale of my house. However, I have to believe that I am being guided to the best possible outcome if it has not sold yet and there has to be a good reason for that. I'm now coming to see more than ever, that when things don't unfold as I think they should, there always seems to be something better coming down the road for me. I can never see it at the time, however.

This includes potential relationships. I honestly don't know whether to give up in this area and call it a day or keep an open mind. You would think that, after two marriages, a failed near death experience and the loss of what had been a really great relationship, I'd say, "Okay, that's it. The Monk's life for me."

I think that when we have a busy family life with our adult children and our grandkids, it will take care of a lot of emotional needs. When I don't have that kind of interaction (because my older adult children are extremely busy and living in two countries), it doesn't afford me that opportunity.

My two youngest children are 25 and 24. Not the age where they really want to be hanging out with Dad, if you catch my drift. Not that they don't love hanging out with me at times. They do. Brendan, my youngest son worked with me for the last few years, and it was amazing, by and large.

As I sit here editing this, my son Brendan and his girlfriend Cailin have been with me for the past week, and it has been wonderful. We will celebrate Brendan's 25th birthday tomorrow, October 9th, by having dinner at the top of Grouse Mountain. The next day he and Cailin will drive back to Toronto. How lucky was I to have been able to do that with my son and his girlfriend? I would say very lucky indeed, as a family is the most important gift we will ever have in our lives. This is something that took a very long time for me to learn. As this step suggests, I try to be a powerful example to both of them that having the faith I do is working in my life.

Living Alone But Not Lonely

When you are on your own, life feels different. I am currently spending a lot of time alone. I have no television and only Netflix on my computer. Fortunately I love to read. My new apartment in West Vancouver is sparsely furnished as I await the sale of my furnished home in Ontario. Consequently I have very little in my place except for two chairs and a bed from IKEA. As a result, this apartment is like a monk's quarters, which given my relationship status, may be quite appropriate! Very Zen.

I brought a number of posters from my Toronto residence/edit suite that reminds me of my past successes. Right across from the chair I'm sitting in is the poster of *The Grey Fox* and next to it a full-page article from the Vancouver Province, written in 1980. There is a picture of my late business associate, Phillip Borsos, with the headline, "Borsos Shooting Miner's Tale". I have the poster for *Yonge Street, Toronto Rock & Roll Stories,* a series that we recently did for CTV/Bravo! with an article from the National Post newspaper. Next to it is another poster of my last production of *Super Volcano, Yellowstone's Fury* that will air in 2014 on the Smithsonian Channel in the United States.

Beside that poster of Yonge Street are two covers from the Toronto Star Week and the T V Times about one of our productions, which aired on CBC and HD Net in the United States.

Remember the Covenant and My Mercedes?

By the way, I just got a call from the mechanic. Instead of $4000, the bill will be roughly $600 to fix my turbo charger.

Does this prove Master Mind's existence, or that I have a covenant because I prayed and released the outcome to Its guidance? It clearly didn't hurt. It does further affirm that if I continue to believe, trust and ask for guidance, I get it. I can also even ask for help around money because I do want to pay off all my current creditors and investors. I believe with my covenant I will be guided.

What I would like to do

I also want to be of service with my writing and speaking. What I do know is that if my heart is in the right place, there is no doubt in my mind that I will be guided to the right outcome.

Risk Failure

Today I had a chance to guide my students through an exercise in class. The purpose was to point out how important it is to take risks, and risk failure. Those crushing defeats I had in the past have been the very catalysts that have generated the greatest positive changes in my life.

It's important to risk letting go of perfectionism and fear and to embrace change. I believe these qualities apply to all our lives regardless of our age. We have to be willing to put ourselves out there. If we think about it, what have we really got to lose?

We're all headed for the departure lounge at some point. Do we want to get there and say, "Damn, why didn't I say hello to that person? Why didn't I try and write my memoirs? Why didn't I tell my spouse how much I loved her? Why didn't I tell my children how important they were to me and that I loved them? Why didn't I ski that double black diamond run? Why didn't I get a new Triumph Bonneville when I wanted to?"

Furthermore, why didn't I forgive my friend for hurting my feelings all those years ago – so long ago I can't even remember why I got angry – and why haven't I spoken to them in years? My mind says, "I'm not going to be the one to pick up the phone." PICK IT UP before it's too late.

Take a chance. Risk failure. Risk rejection. Risk success. If you find yourself in a place of depression or loneliness, then it's imperative to reach out to others. It is often said that there is always someone in worse shape than you, so reach out to them too. Volunteer at a soup kitchen for the homeless. Help other seniors who are unable to leave their homes or apartments. There are so many great opportunities out there.

Have you always been interested in creative endeavours? Join the local amateur theatre, writing group, poetry enthusiasts, or fine arts group. Initially you may feel nervous if you don't know anyone. Can you remember when you were anxious and shy on your first day of school? Oh my, how we worried about being judged because we were so self-conscious of our age, physique, looks or histories. Some of us just lacked the core confidence to get out there.

If we have a Master Mind group, we are blessed and thus able to get active in so many ways. It gives us all a chance to be of service. True happiness really does come from being of service.

What about living in a manner that sets the highest example for those around you? Have you ever noticed those folks that are generally always happy regardless of their circumstances? They are powerful examples to us as to how to act. If we are chronically unhappy old men and women, people will run from us like the plague. Who wants to be around someone who is negative, judgmental, full of self-pity and mean? Not me. Here is a quote from a friend of mine whose spiritual guru said to him in the depths of his existential angst, "You are drowning in your own shit. You smell so bad that nobody wants to be around you."

I don't know how anyone could be clearer in their communication about their own place in life when they are in that negative frame of mind. In honor of my friend Bill, I suggest we all continue to pray for humility.

Humility is a wonderful gift and within it are the seeds of true happiness. It's also imperative to have a gratitude list. Regardless of where we are in our lives, and what difficulties we've had to face and /or overcome, if we sit down and do an honest reflection with others, we will be able to look back on our lives and realize just how blessed we've been.

Proof of Faulty Filer & Imperfection

As I have previously shared with you, my 'faulty filter', is one of my primary character defects. It turns out the building manager where I live has not painted the parking lot wall on the ground level for years. They painted it yesterday and removed all the reference numbers. I've been here and parking in the same spot about three weeks. I came out his morning to find a note on my car because I had apparently parked in the wrong location. The note was fairly lengthy and suggested that I didn't know that the parking was reserved and paid for.

I've been parking beside this car for the past three weeks. The owner of the car doesn't live in my complex, but works at a retail store right next to the entrance to our parking lot. They can see that there are now no clear markings on the wall. How do I react? My first thought is to write them an equally moronic (in my opinion) note:

Dear Mr./Ms. Perfection. I aspire to be as intelligent as you one day. Wow, I'm so glad you were there to let me know that where I was parking was paid parking and reserved too. (I would have thought normally for residents of our complex – not sales associates), but, obviously I was just too dimwitted to realize that and I can't tell you how grateful I am that you pointed out my imperfection and lack of temporal and spatial cognitive skills. I grovel before your insight and wisdom. Please, please just go propagate yourself and die! Oops. This is why I will share my story with you and not the driver. Hopefully, in spite of my lapse of judgment on my profanity, you will still find me a positive example, in spite of my obvious imperfections.

The fact is that I practiced humility and restraint of both pen and tongue, which is a positive step for me. I really believe that it is progress, not perfection that we should be pursuing. Perfectionism is a major flaw that plagues so many of us and causes such pain.

Progress, Not Perfection

You would think after the previous paragraphs on how to clear out the faulty filter, practice humility and restraint of pen and tongue, I would sort of be a spiritual giant, wouldn't you? Well, guess what I just did (it really is progress not perfection)? In a moment devoid of any humility or sound judgment I started to I read an article by a well-known Canadian television journalist, John Doyle. He is the television critic for Canada's national newspaper, the Globe & Mail. Now, I can't say that John is any great fan of mine, but on a few occasions he has spoken kindly about some of my productions. But I do love his writing. The article was about the sorry state of Canadian broadcasting and lamenting the race to the bottom (as it were – my words). He went on to point out the absolute mediocrity of the executives running Canadian broadcasting (and primarily the Canadian Broadcasting Corporation). In a moment of what I felt to be divine inspiration, I thought, what the hell. I should let the executive who turned down my series idea for CANUSA Lodge know what I really think of his abilities and skills.

Then, with the trumpets and sirens of insanity screeching in my head, I thought, I might as well let the President and the new

Executive Vice President of the CBC know just exactly how fed up I am. As far as I'm concerned, they should just go ahead and shut the whole bloated bureaucracy down. (In the background will be a lot of Conservatives howling with glee and hoping my message is heard).

My reasoning has primarily to do with the pursuit of creative excellence. CBC is <u>not</u> a commercial broadcaster. Needless to say, my friend and legal counsel for 30 years who read what I thought was a brilliant missive, said, " I just got a strong whiff of your bridge burning in Toronto even though you are sitting five thousand kilometers away in Vancouver." While my delivery lacked a certain degree of subtlety, I still stand by my comments.

A Little Cheese With That Whine

Today is my second day out of bed. I got a very severe flu last Thursday night. That was a week ago today. I still got up Friday and went swimming again, but I didn't feel right. I went to meet some friends Saturday morning and worked with a fellow who asked me for help with his finances. We got together and talked about where he was in life. Then we looked at what steps he might take to start correcting his thinking and behaviour around money and debting.

As seniors, (I hate that word) we need to be aware of these respiratory illnesses. I can set an example for others by insuring I practice good self-care. I really don't have anyone out here that I can call yet.

Fortunately for me my son Brendan arrived on Sunday night from Vancouver Island. He's now been with me for five days. That was a real blessing, and I was able to really enjoy my time with him. I did try to get up and go to dinner with him, but all I did was cough up a storm and not enjoy any of my food. But it was nice to spend time with him.

What I notice when I get sick is that I don't do sick "well". I tend to be rather immature. If there is anyone around to listen, I willingly moan and groan about how bad I feel. I don't know if it's a "male" thing or what.

I find it hard to ask anyone for guidance when I'm sick too. My conscious contact seems to evaporate. I struggle with prayer and meditation. It doesn't really come too easily to me in this state, even in the best of times. As I may have indicated in the past, I have a mind that is rather quick. I use to say, "I even sleep fast". My mind just spins at a very high RPM. The trouble is that sometimes it doesn't go anywhere, except when it tells me, "Okay, this is it. You're on the way out. You know you have the new MERS (replacing SARS). And by the way, that pneumonia shot you paid two or three hundred bucks for didn't work." My mind just goes to worst-case scenario-izing and catastrophizes. It is often my default setting

Not to beat an idea to death, but my mind is like one of those restaurant wheels where the waiter places the order, and the chef then turns the wheel endlessly to read the next slip.

My mind is analogous to that wheel and just keeps spinning and looking to the next thought to worry about. I can ask the Master Mind's guidance and just chill out and wait for answers to materialize. I'm learning that I need to be patient. The Master Mind is not a short order cook, for me at least.

If we are open to the Master Mind, then many wonderful things seem to come my way. All my disability insurance claims have now been approved. My car is fixed. My son is here. I am at peace ninety per cent of the time. I seem to be doing well in most areas of my life.

What I really need to do is lock down my formal Master Mind Group.

Master Mind Success

> Saturday, October 18, 2013.
> We had our first Master Mind meeting this morning. There were three of us - Mike, Jey and me.

Try, Try Again

I submitted a number of new projects to broadcasters over the past two months. As of last week (second week of January, 2014) they were all turned down. I do feel a sense of acceptance now that my days of producing network television appear to be over. I trust that I am being guided to the best outcome. I choose to no longer hold out false hope that this area of my life is going to change. It's not worth the emotional turmoil I keep going through in submitting these ideas and then being rejected. Regardless of that news, I do feel peace of mind because of the Eight Steps.

Hope Springs Eternal

I am beginning to feel a renewed sense of hope. I know from first hand experience that I do have a message of hope to share with others. I intend to use that gift of writing and speaking be of service and assist others like myself who have found themselves at a turning point in life and are not certain which path to follow.

I want to tell all of you about an amazing therapy I am doing called Neurofeedback. Here is how it is described in Wikipedia.

Neurofeedback is a type of biofeedback that measures brain waves to produce a signal that can be used as feedback on brain activity to teach self-regulation. Neurofeedback is commonly provided using video or sound, with positive feedback for desired brain activity and negative feedback for brain activity that is undesirable. The most accurate form of neurofeedback is the one guided by qEEG that is usually used in clinical settings.

What I do is see a clinician, Linda Bailey, who was trained as a Registered Nurse and works out of her own clinic in North Vancouver. The neuroscientists, who created the program, trained Linda, and I've been seeing her on average twice a week for about four months.

My analogy for Neurofeedback is that it is like using the disk repair tool on my Mac Book Air. That software repairs the damaged files on the hard drive. In this case, my hard drive is analogous to my brain and the neurofeedback is literally repairing and rebooting my brain.

I have now undergone thirty sessions. As a result of this therapy, I have been able to cease taking all of my medications. My anxiety level has dropped significantly. I am able to focus better. I am just so grateful that my friend Richard led me to this. He was in my Master Mind group in Ontario. Richard used neurofeedback to overcome post-traumatic stress disorder.

As a result of the neurofeedback, I would say that right here, right now I feel peace of mind and I believe you can too.

More good news! I received a telephone call last night from Los Angeles. I spoke to the former head of Zig Ziegler's production company for one-hour. He has invited me to join in on a new online broadcasting opportunity being created in the United States. It will launch in ten major markets and is headquartered in Los Angeles. Its sole purpose will be to broadcast positive, affirming and enlightening programming. Here is the link to it.

http://www.myimaginetv.com

In addition, they would like to be able to assist us in the marketing of my talks and books. They are also interested in broadcasting and selling the various televisions shows we've produced over the years. They've sent me a contract, and we've agreed on the terms. This opportunity does give me options so I am not so dependent on just producing network television. I can now also focus on producing my own talks, corporate, inspirational, motivational and spiritual. That is something I've always wanted to do.

I've now spoken to my associates at the university, and they are going to help me out with two cameras and two of the students in cinematography will shoot this for me. I've spoken to a few of my screenwriting students who will act as my crew. This will be film production 101. I'm back to where I started thirty years ago.

To Wrap Up Our Journey

Could I have planned this? I'm not sure whether I could have ever dreamt of something like this happening. It is literally like a Hollywood movie with a happy ending. I will have to let you know how it works out financially but I know that I have enough for today.

What I have learned through this journey that I've just taken is that I do have value as a human being. If we really do let go of old self-defeating thinking and beliefs about ourselves and ask for help we will get it. I have also learned that I am long way from perfection and that I really need to learn to love myself warts and all.

I also believe that prosperity includes the richness of family and friends and a relationship with a Higher Power of your choice. All the money in the world is meaningless, if we don't have someone to share it with.

It is my sincere belief that you too will find whatever it is you are looking for if you will follow these simple Eight Steps.

I want to thank you personally for taking the time and investing your money in buying this book, and I pray you will find all the happiness and purpose you have been seeking for your own life. I would love to hear from any of you if you are willing to contact me and let me know about your journey. You can email me at davidbradybooks@gmail.com

It is my heartfelt prayer that each and every one of you will be guided to the greatest good that you could have ever hoped for and that you too will find the way to overcome adversity, find peace of mind, prosperity and a conscious contact with the Master Mind of your choice, who will supply you with everything you need to live your life as you always desired.

CPSIA information can be obtained at www.ICGtesting.com
Printed in the USA
BVOW09s1654250914

368127BV00011B/567/P